25 Years of Emancipation?

Joy Charnley, Malcolm Pender,
Andrew Wilkin (eds.)

25 Years of
Emancipation?

Women in Switzerland
1971-1996

Peter Lang • Bern

Die Deutsche Bibliothek – CIP-Einheitsaufnahme

25 years of emancipation?
Women in Switzerland 1971-1996 /
Joy Charnley ... (ed.) – Bern : Lang, 1997
ISBN 3-906759-65-2

301.4120 9494

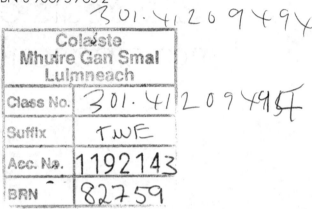
Published with the aid of the Arts Council of Switzerland
Pro Helvetia and the University of Strathclyde

US-ISBN 0-8204-3428-0
ISBN 3-906759-65-2

Foreword by the Swiss Ambassador

It gives me great pleasure to write some introductory words to the present volume, *25 Years Emancipation? Women in Switzerland 1971–1996,* which contains the papers given at the conference of the same title held in the University of Strathclyde from 29th to 31st March 1996. 1996 marked both the two hundredth anniversary of the founding of the University and also the twenty-fifth anniversary of the introduction of female suffrage at federal level in Switzerland. The conference was not only a fitting celebration of these two anniversaries, however, but was also the most significant collaboration between the Department of Modern Languages at the University, Pro Helvetia (the Swiss Council of the Arts) and the Swiss Embassy in London. Co-operation between the three in the development of Swiss Studies in the Department of Modern Languages goes back many years and has taken many forms, and it was thus highly appropriate, at a time of increased awareness of the history of women and of their present role in society, that a conference on this topic should take place at the University of Strathclyde. It therefore gave me great pleasure to accept the invitation of the Principal of the University of Strathclyde, Professor John Arbuthnott, to join him in opening the conference. That the conference was seen as important is evidenced, firstly, by the fact that women prominent in Swiss life found time to participate and give papers, secondly, by the enthusiastic response of those who attended and participated in the discussions, and thirdly, by the publication of this volume which will make the material of the conference available to an even wider public.

François Nordmann

Table of Contents

Joy Charnley, Malcolm Pender, Andrew Wilkin

Introduction

Since the early 1990s the French, German and Italian Divisions of the Department of Modern Languages at the University of Strathclyde each has a member whose research interests lie in Swiss culture: Joy Charnley (French), Malcolm Pender (German), Andrew Wilkin (Italian). As far as we know, no other university in the United Kingdom has specialist cover in this way of the three main cultures of Switzerland, and this was a welcome development in the Department's long-established Swiss connections. For, since the late 1970s, many Swiss writers have visited us and there have been many study and research visits from the Department to Swiss libraries and archives, and in March 1989 a conference was organised with the title *Change and Continuity in Switzerland*, the proceedings of which were published. During this time, good relations were established with the Pro Helvetia Foundation and with the Swiss Embassy in London, and it was therefore appropriate, when the opportunity arose, for the three of us to enhance the existing Swiss components to teaching and research. Over the last three years, we have thus supplemented our Swiss Honours programmes, introduced an option, *The Cultures of Switzerland*, into the BA Honours in European Studies, increased, with the help of Pro Helvetia, holdings in the Library on Swiss matters, and moved towards co-ordinating our individual research.

1996 marked the 200th anniversary of the founding of the University of Strathclyde and the 25th anniversary of the introduction of female suffrage at federal level in Switzerland. This double anniversary presented an ideal opportunity for us to bring our joint interest in Switzerland and Swiss studies to a wider public by mounting a conference here to take stock of changes in the position of women in Swiss society over a quarter of a century. The theme of the conference would also make a contribution to increasing general interest in the history and role of women in society, and we were pleased to be able to add to the work being done in this field. We wished to underline the investigative nature of the conference and also to indicate that the road to emancipation is long and hard and that freedom is not won by the simple introduction of the vote. It therefore seemed appropriate to include a question mark in the title so that the conference would be seen not simply to record, but also to evaluate the period under discussion: *25 Years Emancipation? Women in Switzerland 1971–1996.* The University, the Swiss Embassy in London and Pro Helvetia all reacted enthusiastically to our draft proposals and provided help and support as the conference took shape. The Glasgow Film Theatre welcomed our approach to them and made arrangements, also with the help of Pro Helvetia, for a presentation of Swiss films by women directors in conjunction with the conference, and for the personal appearance of the director Patricia Plattner.

The Conference ran from 29 to 31 March 1996. The presence of the Principal of the University of Strathclyde, Professor John Arbuthnott and of his wife Dr Elinor Arbuthnott and the presence of the Swiss Ambassador to the United Kingdom, His Excellency M. François Nordmann and Mme Miriam Nordmann to perform the opening ceremony, indicated both the importance of Swiss studies at the University and the importance of the subject of the conference. Dr Arbuthnott stressed in her introduction that Anderson's Institution – the nucleus of what was later to become the University – admitted women to higher education in 1796, a unique situation for the time. The subsequent range of speakers – all women – testified both to the progress made in the social status of women in Switzerland since 1971 and to the importance of the role they now play there in public life. It was fitting that the first and last papers of the conference should be given by two politicians from different parties occupying prominent positions from which they influence the course of Swiss public life: Rosemarie Simmen, elected member of the Swiss Upper House and President of Pro Helvetia, set the framework for the deliberations which were to follow by identifying the formal steps for improving the status of women which have been taken since 1971 and those which still require to be taken; and Yvette Jaggi, Mayoress of Lausanne, concluded the proceedings with a perspective on the role of women and the challenges which they face in Swiss society in years to come. Women academics, whose research and publications inform the content and influence the tenor of public debate, had also accepted invitations to review the twenty-five year period from their professional point of view: Brigitte

Studer and Regina Wecker examined the history of the women's movement in Switzerland and the development of the political momentum towards the affirmative vote in 1971; Elisabetta Pagnossin Aligasakis and Annelies Debrunner discussed the contemporary role of women in Swiss society, particularly in relation to political involvement and to the workforce; and Agnès Cardinal, Beatrice von Matt and Erika Swales examined aspects of women's writing in Switzerland since 1971. Under this last heading, we were particularly pleased that three Swiss women writers – Anne Cuneo, Amélie Plume and Isolde Schaad – found time to attend and to participate in a round-table discussion. This took the form of an open debate, which was chaired by the Scottish writer Liz Lochhead, on the problems of writing in a small country, and sought to explore parallels between Switzerland and Scotland: both small countries, both having cultures which exist in the shadow of larger neighbours, both experiencing problems of political and cultural identity. All four writers read extracts from their publications in their own languages, and provided in this way an interesting flavour of their work. During the round-table discussion, as indeed during all other sessions of the conference, there was lively and interested participation by the audience, and the generally enthusiastic response to the course of the conference confirmed that its theme was topical and relevant.

We are glad that the papers given by such a noted representative group of women in public life in Switzerland are now being published, and we are grateful to the contributors for making them available to us. We are also delighted to include the text of an interview with Patricia Plattner. Additionally, we have included two essays which were not delivered at the conference but which serve to complete the picture of women's writing in Switzerland. We feel that the volume as a whole reflects the extent to which Swiss women have caught up with their other European counterparts, and have in certain ways overtaken some of them. For example, Switzerland now has a higher percentage of women in parliament than either France or the United Kingdom.

Following on the success of the conference, we were granted permission by the Faculty of Arts and Social Sciences of the University of Strathclyde to set up a Centre for Swiss Cultural Studies. The Centre will act as the formal focal point for existing activities and will additionally promote activity in three areas: in publication (the present volume is the first to appear under the aegis of the Centre and it is envisaged that occasional short monographs and thematically-linked collections of essays will follow); in research (where it is hoped to build on the existing base of postgraduate work); and in contacts and exchanges (the Centre will strengthen existing links and help to create new ones). The conference was thus crucial in formalising the status of Swiss Studies at the University of Strathclyde.

We should like to thank very much indeed all those who participated in the conference and who helped to make it such a stimulating event. We should like also to thank Pro Helvetia and the University of Strathclyde for the generous financial support which enabled the conference to take place. Our thanks also go to everyone who helped in the organisation of the conference, in particular Professor Arthur Midwinter, Dean of the Faculty of Arts and Social Sciences, Professor Terry Wade, former Chairman of the Department of Modern Languages, Professor Gordon Millan, current Chairman, and Mrs Janice Wigley, secretary in the Department. We thank Ken Ingles, Director of the Glasgow Film Theatre, and Vanessa Paynton, its Education Officer. Finally, we would like to thank Pro Helvetia and the University of Strathclyde for the financial support which made this publication possible.

University of Strathclyde
May 1997

Rosemarie Simmen

Women in Switzerland since 1971:
Major Achievements – Minor Changes?

Introduction

Major Achievements – Minor Changes? That is what the Federal Commission for Women's Issues called their survey of where women stand in Switzerland after 25 years of suffrage and the twentieth anniversary of the Commission. I have chosen it as the motto for my remarks because, try as I might to think up a better title, I could find none that even came close to capturing the situation so succinctly.

I shall start my paper with a brief look at past developments and a progress report on the position of women in Switzerland; the second part will offer some insight into practical matters with reference to three specific areas – politics, education with a glance at the economy, and culture and the media; and in the third and final section I should like to venture some perspectives on the future.

History

Is there such a thing as 'women's issues'? Whether the answer is yes or no depends on how we understand the question. Yes! Of course there are questions that relate particularly to women. But if the notion of 'women's issues' targets matters relating exclusively to women, then the answer is a clear No! In that sense there is no such thing.

All so-called women's issues concern society at large: they cut across all areas of politics and the changes they generate affect both sexes. The only feature specific to women's issues is that they affect women more or differently than they do men. I hope you will keep this in mind as you consider the facts and ideas I shall present to you.

To examine a development, we must first decide on a starting point. That choice is always arbitrary, because history is an ongoing process. But even ongoing processes have their occasional highlights, and it makes sense to begin our observations on women's emancipation in

Switzerland at just such a point: the year 1971. Not because before that Switzerland's women were pitiful creatures living in a form of modern slavery, but because that is the year universal suffrage was introduced at the federal level. The right to vote and to stand for office is crucial to a modern democracy: a modern democracy that does not ensure *all* of its citizens the right to participate in elections and plebiscites is no longer conceivable today. At the threshold of the 21st century, the fact that in Classical Greece, the mother of all democracies, democracy was not all-inclusive can no longer serve as an explanation, much less an excuse, for only partial suffrage.

A number of milestones have been achieved over the last 25 years. Here are the most important ones:

7 February 1971: Suffrage extended to women at the federal level;

28 January 1976: Establishment of the Federal Commission for Women's Issues – a commission originally composed of an equal number of men and women and later, sadly, with women in the majority, not because of any claims to female hegemony but because of a lack of male interest;

14 June 1981: Approval of the Equal Rights Amendment (Article 4, Clause 2 of the Federal Constitution);

1 January 1988: Implementation of new marriage laws, bringing equal rights for husband and wife, and equal status for paid work and work done to benefit family members;

24 March 1995: Passage by Parliament of a law guaranteeing equal legal status to men and women; as there has been no referendum launched against it, it comes into force on 1 July 1996.

Development

Much has undoubtedly changed for the better over the past years. Women have gained strength and self-confidence; they have become increasingly aware that they often work harder than men, but that what they do in the home, at their jobs and in the field of public service does not receive due recognition. Women work together more than they used to, formulating common needs and undertaking important grass-roots and networking tasks. Time and again, cross-party coalitions of women are formed in the federal and cantonal parliaments when matters of particular concern to women are at issue, for example maternity insurance.

But all these positive developments notwithstanding, we cannot overlook the fact that economic, social and political equality of the sexes is still a long way off. It appears that success in this sector can be attained only through a series of innumerable small steps, and sometimes it almost seems as if the same issues and demands keep coming up again and again, able to find neither rest nor a solution.

For example, women are massively under-represented in politics, and though the number of women candidates has risen significantly, a woman's chances of election are always far worse than a man's.

At the workplace, most women are victims of the glass ceiling, unable to advance past middle management; wage discrimination and a low assessment of traditional women's occupations remain the order of the day, and lower salaries mean lower retirement pensions. Women have taken on new tasks and responsibilities in society and the state; unfortunately a comparable trend among men in the home has been rather sluggish. There are still so few 'new-style' fathers as to render them a negligible quantity; and even where we find them, we can often observe a great discrepancy between the ideal and reality. Not every modern young father turns out to be as open and co-operative as he considers himself to be. And that is not even entirely his fault. Because existing social, employment and family policies are not only unconducive to new ideas, they hamper them dramatically and may even obstruct them altogether.

All in all, the questioning tone of the title *Major Achievements – Minor Changes?* is justified. So let me now move on to the second section, where I will home in on a few selected areas and examine them more closely.

Politics in a Broad Sense

Many people think politics is the activity that takes place in the various legislative bodies of the land: in Switzerland that would mean in the federal, cantonal and communal parliaments. That is true, but only to a degree – politics as the exercise of a political mandate is only what one might call the tip of an iceberg. Below it lies a far larger field of

political activity, part of which is entrusted to the Federal Commission
for Women's Issues. Created as an extra-parliamentary commission in
1976, it was the Federal Council's response to a variety of proposals and
recommendations. The Commission deals with a wide range of policy
issues relevant to women: it takes stands on proposed draft bills and parliamentary initiatives, performs tasks entrusted to it by the Federal Council
or government departments, drafts its own recommendations, tables motions, monitors the effectiveness of measures taken and, at intervals, pub-
lishes reports on topics relating to women from all walks of life.

Probably the best-known of these reports was published in 1980
under the title *Nehmen Sie Platz, Madame. Die politische Repräsentation
der Frauen in der Schweiz* (Take a Seat, Madam. Political Representation
of Women in Switzerland) and deals with the under-representation of
women in politics. Less charitable minds might think it appropriate to
subtitle the publication 'Move Over, Sir' as the real problem for many
men is not that they grudge women seats in parliament, but that they
find it difficult to accept the fact that every seat occupied by a woman
is no longer available to a man.

Naturally the Commission for Women's Issues is also responsible for
the preparatory and follow-up work relating to UN World Women's
Conferences. And it is partner and adviser to the Equal Rights Bureaux
of the Confederation and the cantons. As the Swiss cantons possess a
great deal of autonomy, factual equality of the sexes is impossible, or at
least impracticable, without their co-operation. This autonomy also explains why conditions in the single cantons vary so. While this diversity is in one way a handicap, it also offers women enormous opportunities, as the cantonal parliaments alone account for altogether about
3000 seats, which amounts to nearly half of the total number of seats
in the regional legislatures of the European Union. This fact leads me
to my next heading.

Politics in the Narrow Sense

In terms of politics in the narrow sense, 1971 was the crucial year. It was
then, as mentioned above, that women received the right to vote at the
federal level, several cantons having already set a good example within
the framework of their own authority. The introduction of universal

national suffrage required acceptance by both the majority of the still exclusively male electorate and the majority of cantons. By Swiss law a decision at the parliamentary or government level, as might have been made in an indirect democracy, would not have been enough. That provides some explanation of why women received the right to vote at such a late date: the electorate is traditionally more conservative than Parliament and the government in Switzerland does not have a monopoly on change. (The situation is, incidentally, similar with respect to Switzerland's role in Europe. Once again it is the voters, rather than Parliament and the government, who are not – yet? – ready for change.) There is an old saying that though the Swiss may get up late, they can run fast. That still seems to apply, because when it comes to women in Parliament and government, we have already caught up with the European norm – partly because we are making progress and partly because progress in most other countries is equally slow, sometimes even slower than in Switzerland.

But a great deal remains to be done. For example, we must systematically eliminate the major obstacles to the election of women, one of which is their under-representation on ballot papers. Certainly the situation is steadily improving, and virtually no political party can afford to enter an election without women on its list. The single exception is the Freedom Party, and that is probably because it started life as the Automobile Party, and there are – fortunately – very few women who would consider cars a sufficient basis for a political programme. But preparing party lists with a bias towards women continues to be a touchy subject in other parties as well. There are so many possibilities, from setting up separate men's and women's lists to introducing compulsory quotas, making voluntary agreements and taking democratic votes on numbers at delegates' meetings.

And speaking of quotas, although they may have a recognised place in Swiss political life, particularly in constituting party committees, they have not yet been able to assert themselves in parliamentary or government elections. All in all, it would be justified to say that the Social Democratic Party, and above all the Greens, have the edge over the conservative parties with regard to the ratio of women to men.

The number of women candidates on election lists is one aspect of the problem, their chances of election is another, because women who have made it onto the ballot tend to do worse than their male colleagues. In 1991, one out of 24 women candidates was elected, while among men it was one out of 11. In other words, a woman candidate's chances of election were not even half as great as her male counterpart's. Once again there are differences between parties, and once again the left/ Green parties are ahead of the right.

Education

In Switzerland, education is historically a mainly cantonal responsibility. The Swiss Federal State was the successor to a centuries-old alliance that ceased to exist in 1798 and was not replaced by a modern federal state until 1848, 50 years later. But 150 years of federal state have still not produced a genuinely centralised system, and the cantons continue to guard their rights jealously, making sure the balance does not tilt more than absolutely necessary towards a central power. This is in no way discreditable and, in view of the trend towards regionalisation and federalisation in Europe, absolutely up-to-date. But it results in an enormous, and for outsiders sometimes confusing, range of differences, for example in the school system. The Conference of Education Ministers, the co-ordinating body of the cantons, has issued very forward-looking guidelines for dealing even-handedly with girls and boys. The way the cantons translate them into practice varies and is probably about average for Europe. But this theoretically attractive diversity can prove awkward when it comes to the modalities of daily life, a point I shall be returning to later. As it is difficult to get a general picture of the situation at the compulsory school level, let me use an example from the university level to demonstrate how much remains to be done in the field of equal opportunity. Switzerland was once a pioneer when it came to women attending university. In 1867 the University of Zürich became the first place of higher learning, apart from Paris, to admit a woman – a Russian – to its medical studies programme. By the beginning of this century the proportion of women students had risen to 25 per cent, but only thanks to the many foreign women who opted for Switzerland and its liberal atmosphere. Swiss women were in the minority and when foreigners began to stay away, the proportion of women fell rapidly and would not regain the 25 per cent mark of 1906 until the 1970s.

Since then women have been catching up. Almost half of the school-leaving certificates qualifying for university entrance go to women, and women account for 40 per cent of the student population at institutes of higher learning. But let us not rejoice too soon, because what happens during and after university gives grounds for concern. While 50 per cent of all women are eligible to go to university, only 40 per cent of these women actually do; one third of the women who begin studying conclude their academic careers with a diploma or licentiate, so that by the time doctoral exams come round, only one quarter of the candidates are women. Women account for only 4 per cent of Switzerland's professors, and in 1994 the University of St Gall was still an all-male preserve.

Figures like these always give rise to a host of programmes for the advancement of women – women's delegates, women's programmes, encouragement schemes, rights of appeal for rejected candidates, special grants, etc. etc. But with universities too experiencing lean times, measures of this kind tend to be particularly at risk, and competition for grants has become even more relentless than usual. Moreover, as indispensable as such measures are, they are not enough.

And that brings me back to the subject of school, under the heading of timetables. The system found above all in German-speaking Switzerland today plays nasty tricks on women who would like jobs that demand more than a few odd hours per day. There is still no such thing as a standard timetable. Whoever has more than one child at school may easily find that, by the time the last child has left for school in the morning, the first is already on the way home. All-day schools – still the exception – tend to be the preserve of private-sector education. That makes it extremely difficult for most mothers to plan their days sensibly; and if they do go out to work, worrying about whether everything is all right at home is anything but conducive to concentration. As compulsory schooling is a cantonal matter, possibilities vary from canton to canton, with progressive and stone-age cantons cheek by jowl.

On balance, working women are still faced with an uphill struggle, and too many of them continue to attempt the impossible feat of being all things to all people, at work and at home. Women in unskilled, poorly paid jobs are the ones who suffer most, because they do not even have the comfort of job satisfaction. But even highly qualified professions, be they in the scientific or the economic sector, pose problems. In both, women in top positions are the rare exception, and as long as the framework remains as unfavourable as it is now, the likelihood of change is, sadly, nil.

Though this situation has been recognised and criticised for years, I had a disturbing experience not long ago that really brought its practical effects home to me. In connection with a symposium about women and science, I visited one of the chemical companies in Basle known for its exemplary policies towards women. I had a chance to speak at length with eight top-ranking researchers from various scientific fields and all continents but Africa. Not one of these women was Swiss! All of them agreed that there were certainly Swiss women graduates – extremely promising ones – who embarked on scientific careers. But most of them left their jobs sooner or later – often for family reasons, or sometimes to move into different professions, particularly public relations. The researchers I spoke to mentioned three reasons for this:

1) Their Swiss women colleagues could not cope with the burden of having both a profession and a family, despite favourable employment conditions like annual hours, a flexible range of part-time employment, salaries enabling them to hire qualified child-minders, etc.;
2) They had partners who could not accept a high-ranking professional woman as a partner;
3) They were not prepared to keep pace with the – admittedly high – demands of a career in research and changed to a softer job.

I don't know whether we Swiss women have a particular problem here and whether this is a specifically Swiss malaise. But the conversation certainly made me think. Now let me turn to the third and final area with which I shall deal.

Culture and the Media

One would think that women had better chances in the cultural field, where the pervasive spirit ought to be different, might I say more cultivated, than in the political and economic sectors. Conversely, one might argue that if women are not well represented in politics and the economy, there is no reason for the cultural scene to form an exception.

There is no question that the women's movement of the Seventies also broke new ground in the cultural landscape, paving the way for the feminist alliances that emerged in diverse fields of the arts and culture in the Eighties: Women's Music Weeks for rock and jazz musicians, a Women's Music Forum for composers of classical music, the Association of Women in the Theatre, etc. Women working in the visual arts have, incidentally, had their own organisation since 1920.

While women were steering a new course in the Seventies, video art was emerging as a new addition to the traditional arts (the cinema, 100 years old now, is, after all, also considered one of the traditional arts). It is probably no coincidence that women found this new art-form, which had no given structures and certainly no structures bearing a male stamp, the easiest field in which to establish themselves. Today Switzerland's women video artists number among the finest in the world.

I have thus far outlined three aspects of a far larger, more complex whole. What conclusions can we draw?

The general goal of equal status for men and women in all areas of society is broadly accepted, at least theoretically. But on a more concrete level, things do not look quite as rosy. The devil is, as they say, in the detail. What is clear is that ensuring equal status for men and women – which often means improving the status of women – is, and remains, a task that cuts through virtually all policy sectors. What are the most important targets?

Family Policy

Social structures must be created to allow fathers and mothers to find forms of living together that do justice to both partners without doing mental, professional or financial damage to their children or themselves. The nuclear family as we know it is one possibility, but there are others, such as extended families of different kinds or single-parent families. The main thing for children is to be able to grow up in a stable environment.

Educational Policy

Very small children are already aware of who is appreciated for what, and will act accordingly. Consequently, adults' behaviour towards children of pre-school age is of crucial importance. At school, the image of men and women conveyed during lessons is central because it cuts across every school subject. The principle of the equality of the sexes must pervade the educational system – from kindergarten right through to universities – as a logical continuation of the parental attitude mentioned above.

Mass Media Policy

The mass media have at least as much influence as school, if not more – an influence that is steadily growing. Television and video images are very powerful in shaping children's views and setting standards that children will take over into their daily lives. This places a heavy burden on the media professionals responsible for programming, but also on parents, who must be familiar with the programmes their children watch so that they can provide explanations or correctives if necessary.

Employment Policies

The work that exists – both paid and unpaid – must be fairly divided among men and women. Who does what job and on what terms is of crucial social significance because it directly determines the esteem a job enjoys. If we take the example of a managerial post versus caring for the aged, you will understand what I mean. The way a job can be done is very important in this context. The complex of conditions involved includes flexible arrangements with regard to working hours for both men and women, equal access to jobs, further education and training, equal prospects of promotion, equal pay for equal work and equal protection against unlawful dismissal. And there is a further aspect we must keep in mind: all these measures notwithstanding, the economy must continue to function properly to guarantee the financial resources a welfare state needs to redistribute to its weaker members.

Social Policy

Social policy is the link between family policy and employment policy. On the one hand it is indispensable as a way of ensuring that families are supplied with a framework that allows paid and unpaid work to be combined with the least possible friction for all concerned. On the other hand a free labour market needs collateral socio-political measures to guarantee the industrial peace that every economy needs if it is to flourish.

Politics

'And what about politics in the narrow sense?', you may ask. Political challenges will not diminish in future, though actual legislative work will be less central, given that, apart from new divorce laws, all the major projects have been dealt with. What the political sector will be required to do is to see to it that equal status for women and men does not become a purely academic concept. It must ensure that the idea of equality is not abused to justify or perpetuate existing inequalities or to downgrade equal status by adjusting to the lowest common denominator.

And there is something else I consider very important. We women have to work harder developing the qualities of long-distance runners. All too often, women who have been voted into office thanks to the enormous efforts and support of other men and women throw in the towel after only a short time. There may be a host of reasons: disappointment at the nature of the work required of them, disappointment at their lack of quick success, disappointment at the amount of energy and commitment demanded from them, etc. In our time, with tenacity at a premium, this blood-letting process does a great deal of practical and psychological damage to women in politics.

As you can see, equality has many faces, and it should never be confused with spurious egalitarianism. To put it in a nutshell: equality of the sexes is not a project that can be completed once and for all and then set aside. It is a process that goes hand in hand with political, social and personal life. And as such it can never be finished – unlike this paper, which I would like to conclude here.

(Translated by Eileen Walliser-Schwarzbart)

REGINA WECKER

The Oldest Democracy and Women's Suffrage: The History of a Swiss Paradox

If it were not such a well-known fact, it would be quite incredible that
– apart from Liechtenstein – Switzerland was the last European country to introduce women's suffrage. In fact, there were important political,
economic, and social factors which might have led us to expect Switzerland to be the nation to set the pace and be among the forerunners
of women's political equality. In the first part of my paper, I shall deal
with this paradoxical development, showing Swiss social, political, and
economic structures and institutions which one might have expected
to advance political equality of women at an early stage. In the second
part I shall try to show how the very same factors – given these specifically Swiss conditions – hampered the realisation of women's suffrage.

The fact that women were enfranchised as late 1971 does not mean
that there were no activities in favour of suffrage. Quite the reverse, in
fact, for from the middle of the nineteenth century onwards the demand
for equality was part of any political agenda. In the nineteenth century,
it occurred only sporadically in connection with the so-called Democratic Movement, which fought for a reform of cantonal constitutions,
with informal groups of women advocating the improvement of the
legal status of women in general.[1] Marie Goegg-Pouchoulin's 'Association internationale des femmes', the first formal association advocating
legal and political equality for women in Switzerland, was founded as
part of an international movement for peace in Geneva in 1868.[2] Since

1 Annamarie Ryter, 'Die Geschlechtsvormundschaft im 19. Jahrhundert', in Mey-
er/Kubli (eds), *Alles was Recht ist* (Liestal: 1992); Beatrix Mesmer, 'Pflichten er-
füllen heisst Rechte begründen', in Studer/Wecker/Ziegler (eds), *Frauen und
Staat. Schweizerische Zeitschrift für Geschichte*, 3, 1996; Beatrix Mesmer, *Ausgeklammert–Eingeklammert. Frauen und Frauenorganisationen in der Schweiz im 19. Jahrhundert* (Basel: 1988); Lotti Ruckstuhl, *Frauen sprengen Fesseln. Hindernislauf zum
Frauenstimmrecht in der Schweiz* (Bonstetten: [n.d.]); Regina Wecker, *Frauen in
der Schweiz. Von den Problemen einer Mehrheit* (Zug: 1983).
2 Compare Susanna Woodtli, *Gleichberechtigung* (Frauenfeld: 1975), pp. 24 ff.

the Women's Congress of 1896 the question of women's political emancipation was broadly discussed. In 1897, Carl Hilty, Professor of Constitutional Law at the University of Berne, published his famous article on the vote,[3] holding that women's suffrage should be introduced
from 'the bottom up', which meant first on the communal level: Switzerland is a federalist country, the cantons being sovereign states within
a state.[4] Thus political decisions are taken on two or even three levels:
on a communal level, individual communities being relatively independent, administrative units[5] deciding on matters such as primary schools
communal buildings, communal road-building, welfare, communal fi-
nances, voting on communal matters; on a cantonal level,[6] the cantons
being responsible for the cantonal bills,[7] dealing with secondary education including universities, health and legal matters, political questions
and institutions such as voting on cantonal matters, plus social and economic questions of the canton; and on the federal level, where a two-
chamber system deals with federal legislation and politics, including the
right to vote on federal matters, international treaties, 'law and order',
the independence of cantonal constitutions and military questions.[8]
Hilty's influential opinion that women's political participation should

3 Carl Hilty, 'Frauenstimmrecht', *Politisches Jahrbuch der Schweizerischen Eidgenos-
   senschaft*, 11, 1897, pp. 245 ff.
4 'The cantons are sovereign within the bonds of the Federal Constitution and
   exercise all rights which have not been transferred to the Federation by the
   Federal Constitution' (Art. 3 of the Federal Constitution of 1874).
5 A typical community has a council (executive), elected by the enfranchised citizens of the community, a small administration and a consultative organ, a communal meeting in which every enfranchised citizen may participate. Most decisions are taken by the communal meeting, including fiscal and financial matters, only most important or highly controversial decisions may be decided by
   ballot.
6 A typical canton has a governing council and a parliament, both elected by the
   enfranchised citizens of that canton. Only in the so-called 'Landesgemeinde'
   cantons does this cantonal assembly of all enfranchised citizens of the canton
   exercise the functions of parliament.
7 Before the bill becomes law citizens decide on it by ballot. In some cantons
   all bills are put to the ballot.
8 Both chambers, the National Council ('Nationalrat') and the council of States
   ('Ständerat') have the same powers and duties, Together ('Vereinigte Bundes-
   versammlung') they elect the Federal Government ('Bundesrat'). Parliament

first be established in the communities, dealing with matters of communal autonomy such as school, welfare, and church, led to several petitions by women submitted to communal or cantonal authorities on the matter of women's suffrage before and after World War I.

From 1915 onwards, women's suffrage was discussed regularly on a cantonal level, in the parliaments of the various cantons – resulting in many cantonal plebiscites on this very question. On a national level, the issue became one of the demands of the famous national strike of 1918 along with other issues of democratic representation. These endeavours will be dealt with in the third part of my paper which will discuss the struggle of the women's movement and the long evolution towards suffrage beginning in the nineteenth century and ending shortly after World War II. [9]

1. The Political and Economic Structure of Switzerland – Factors which might Have Advanced Female Emancipation

– Switzerland was among the first countries to concede adult male suffrage and to abolish property qualifications and the prerogative of birth by the Federal Constitution of 1848. [10] While a considerable number of Swiss men were not enfranchised at the beginning of the 19th century, it then became a matter of common consent that class, the region of domicile and religious denomination should not be factors in an exclusion from political rights. This was considered a matter of human rights and justice. It seems to be a small step to include women in this consent.

The communities were proud of their traditionally democratic institutions within which political decisions were taken by an assembly of the citizens ('Gemeindeversammlung'), and where citizens had the

meets for four annual session (12 weeks). In Switzerland only the federal government and most of the members of cantonal governments are professional politicians drawing their income from their office. All the other politicians have another job and draw comparatively moderate expenses and travelling allowances.

9 Brigitte Studer's paper deals with the period after 1945.

10 Federal Constitution Article 4.

right to elect the representatives of their community: the head of the
local administration as well as, for example, the teacher.

— Swiss democracy not only conferred the right to vote but from the
   end of the nineteenth century citizens had acquired the right to accept or reject laws ('Referendum') and to initiate change in the political order by amending the constitution ('Initiative') even on the
   federal level. Exercising political power was not a question of a decision taken every couple of years, but part of everyday life – in which
   it seemed desirable that women should participate. When women
   started petitioning for women's rights and the improvement of wom-
   en's conditions of life in the middle of the nineteenth century, their
   demands were in agreement with the democratic movement as such.
   They directed their petitions to the cantonal constituencies in order
   to make women's rights part of the new constitutions. Their petitions showed that they were well informed about the political scene
   and the formulation of their demands was linked to the on-going political discussion.

   Switzerland and Swiss institutions served as a model democracy for
   other countries or for movements striving for a democratisation of
   their national institutions as, for example, in Germany in 1848, or in
   the United States. Swiss politicians duly provided support. The functioning of the Swiss political system relying on democratic principles and structures became part of Swiss national identity. Swiss people were proud of the 'ancient' element of Swiss direct democracy,
   where the common man had the power to decide political questions.

— Towards the end of the 19th century, the belief prevailed that the
   Swiss state and its institutions were founded in 1291. A combination
   of this founding myth 'Gründungsmythos' with the story of the myth-
   ological figure of Wilhelm Tell (reinforced by Schiller's drama), who
   was said to have defended Swiss freedom and independence, became
   part of the historical mythology of Switzerland – just in time to cel-
   ebrate a centennial in 1891.[11] Wilhelm Tell had his female counterpart in Gertrud Stauffacher, who was said to have advised her hus-

11 See Werner Meyer, *Mythos und Geschichte* (Basel: 1991).

band. Thus even the myth provided the figure of an independent woman involved in politics.

- Associations were an important means of promoting political, economic and social interests in the European revolutionary movement of 1848. Especially in the various German states women organised as well as men striving with revolutionary zeal for their goals, though women organised themselves separately from men. The failure of the revolution forced leading politicians to flee to Switzerland. In some Swiss cantons, those political refugees were highly respected in the middle of the nineteenth century. They could expect asylum in Switzerland and some of them were even granted Swiss citizenship in order to protect them from German or Austrian authorities and their ideas on democracy were highly respected. Although Swiss asylum policy was highly selective and general approval was often contested by political pressure from the German States, Austria and France who demanded that Switzerland surrender the refugees,[12] it became part of the Swiss national image to be a protector of refugees persecuted because of their fight for freedom and democracy.

The Geneva International Women's Association ('Association internationale des femmes'), which is considered the first independent women's movement in Switzerland (founded 1868), was influenced by those circles of émigrés operating from Switzerland which – despite the failure of the 1848 movement – were struggling for better political and social conditions in Europe. The founder of this international women's association, Marie Goegg-Pouchoulin, had married a German revolutionary, who was both engaged in the international peace movement ('Ligue internationale pour la paix et la liberté') and the international labour movement.[13] Armand Goegg was co-editor of a newspaper called 'Les Etats Unis d'Europe', the 'United Nations of Europe'. Marie Goegg supported him in his endeavours but at the same time used his political connections for her own objective, which was to involve women in the international peace movement.

12 See Marc Vuilleumier, *Flüchtlinge und Immigranten in der Schweiz* (Zürich: 1987).
13 See Susanna Woodtli, *Gleichberechtigung. Der Kampf um die politischen Rechte der Frau in der Schweiz* (Frauenfeld: 1975).

Thus, the role of Switzerland as a country which granted political asylum influenced the political climate in favour of women's emancipation. From the very beginning of her small but well-known international organisation, Marie Goegg made it clear that women could only take part in the common struggle for peace on equal terms with men. Her group continued to exercise its influence by petitioning in favour of a law for economic and civil equality for women at the time of the revision of the Federal Constitution. They addressed their petition to the National Council in 1870. In 1872, Julie von May, a Bernese aristocrat, submitted a similar petition. Although she did not ask for the vote, she advocated equality in education, equal pay and an equal right to inherit.

– Switzerland was industrialised early on, and its industry relied on female labour. By the middle of the nineteenth century, about half the factory workers were women. The economic development in Switzerland – its early industrialisation and the importance of trade – furthered women's independence : factory work provided an income independent from one's family. Because of this independence, the so-called 'Geschlechtsvormundschaft', a bizarre form of guardianship, based on gender, was abolished, and unmarried, divorced, and widowed women were now granted the right to trade and to dispose of their own property. Industrialisation and growing mobility furthered the foundation of supra-regional federations of women workers : the first 'Arbeiterinnenvereine' were founded in the 1880s. Industrialisation furthered at the same time bourgeois women's associations which were founded in order to solve the so-called 'social question' ('soziale Frage') as growing poverty among working class families was called. The 'women's question' ('Frauenfrage') became part of the 'social question', and several women's organisations of very different persuasions – ranging from associations for the abolition of prostitution[14] to the so-called 'Schweizerischer Gemeinnütziger Frauenverein'[15]

14 See Annemarie Käppeli, *Sublime croisade. Ethique et politique du féminisme protestante, 1875–1928* (Geneva : 1990).
15 The SFG supported the idea that the social question and the 'women's question' had to be solved by educating women especially in housework and helping them fulfil their 'female duties'.

(SGF) a female group parallel to the influential 'Schweizerische Gemeinnützige Gesellschaft' – came into being. Although their attitude towards suffrage was very different – the SGF, for example, never discussed it publicly – they were a reservoir of female involvement in state affairs.

– School attendance was mandatory for boys and girls, and primary education had not only been free of charge but more or less equal for boys and girls since the nineteenth century. Educating girls was considered important, too. Zürich boasted the first German-speaking university to admit women, and many of the first women doctors in Russia, Germany, England, and the United States held a degree they had acquired at a Swiss university.

– The first woman to take an ordinary degree at a university was the Russian Nadesha Suslowa, who became a physician at the University of Zürich in 1867. Again, her extraordinary achievement was made possible by the specific political situation of that time. The University of Zürich was a comparatively young institution, founded in the 1830s. Many of its professors were part of the circle of émigrés from Germany of democratic persuasion who did not question a woman's right to study. It is obvious that émigrés developed a keen understanding of other 'oppressed groups' and were, therefore, willing to support their aims. Apart from that, women had already attended lectures in Zürich for some time – though not as regular students. When Suslowa wanted to take a degree, this caused some discussion, but was finally granted by the government because of widespread academic support. Usually early female academics formed a 'reservoir' of emancipationist thought.

2. The Very Same Factors Hampering Women's Emancipation

Despite these modern traits of Swiss society and the democratic traditions of Switzerland, women remained in the backward position normally associated with a pre-industrial, feudal society. What were the reasons? Why was Swiss equality only equality among men?

– The fact that men were enfranchised early on proved to be disadvantageous for women. The introduction of the vote for women in other countries was usually combined with the enfranchisement of parts of the male population and with a restructuring of the electoral system. When woman's suffrage was introduced in Britain in 1918, there were groups of men (for example, agricultural workers) who did not have the vote as yet. The Reform Act thus was a general reform in favour of women *and* men. In Switzerland, however, it was exclusively a question of gender. All Swiss men were enfranchised and had to give up the prerogative to the other sex, and this seemed to devalue politics and democracy in their opinion.

– Although women's groups striving for the vote referred to the founding myth and Schiller's Gertrud Stauffacher by calling their group 'Stauffacherinnen', this provided no successful argument. The date itself – 1291 – the first centennial of 1891 and the following annual celebrations stressed the military elements more than later foundation dates (historians consider 1798 or 1848 much more important). Thus women and their participation were excluded.

– The biggest obstacle, however, was the political system, which gave 'the people' the right to decide on matters which other countries resolved by parliamentary decisions. For women's suffrage this meant that – like any other change of the Federal Constitution – the issue was decided at the polls. In the cantons, a majority of enfranchised men decided. On the federal level, a majority of the voters and the cantons had to agree to any change. This made change a very slow process in the best of cases. But unlike other constitutional or legislative changes, those who were most concerned – women that is – had no say in the matter. They had to convince politicians who presented their request to Parliament, which could then present it to the people. Then those interested in the issue had to campaign and convince every single voter – male voter that is. Direct democracy was actually detrimental to women's rights. All attempts to circumvent this difficulty and to by-pass male popular consent by means of re-interpretation of the constitution – in fact women were not explicitly excluded from the vote – were rejected.[16]

16 See Regina Wecker, 'Staatsbürgerrechte, Mutterschaft und Grundrechte', in Studer/Wecker/Zeigler, *Frauen und Staat. Schweizerische Zeitschrift für Geschichte*, 3, 1996.

– There is another disadvantage of democracy in Switzerland: it makes people excessively patient. Groups fight for a change, they collect signatures for an 'Initiative', they work with groups of politicians in favour of change, the issue is put to the vote, they start campaigns and try to convince voters personally, they invest time, and then at the polls, the 'people' say 'Nay' nevertheless. Whom can they blame? No change of government can help, no election, they can only change the people. So they hope for the next time. Normally those who lose a campaign will soon start to prepare for the next one. Concerning women's suffrage, there were many 'next times', and it seemed so logical to have the vote that for all activists – whether they were living in the nineteenth or at the beginning of the twentieth century – victory seemed at hand, a better campaign, more work, more money and then ... Thus women were patient. Besides, they felt obliged to show that they knew the democratic game in order to show themselves worthy of the vote. It is an unwritten law that if you lose a 'democratic' plebiscite you will have to accept the decision and 'understand' the argument of your political adversary. This is part of our political culture. Women could always be convinced to behave well, because they were afraid they would not get another chance. Thus democracy turned down equality.

– The Swiss 'International Women's Association' was very active in the middle of the 19th century on an international level and took an egalitarian stand on this issue; that is, women referred to the innate rights women had as human beings. But this part of the movement relied on very few women. Most of the women's organisations – about a thousand were established in the nineteenth century – inclined to what has been called a 'dualistic ideology', that is, women were considered different from men and having different rights, and even concerning the political institutions the prevailing opinion was that while politics and economics were considered men's prerogative, women should deal with social institutions and were judged responsible for social welfare. This dualistic view allowed them to pretend they were living in a democratic nation.

– Even when women demanded equal rights, they were very often not talking about the vote, but aimed at equal economic rights, for example, an equal share in an inheritance, equality concerning property rights and economic freedom, which in particular applied to business women having the right to sell and to sign contracts without the consent of either a husband or a guardian. From a pragmatic point of view, these rights seemed more important than the vote – especially in an industrialised country, where more and more women lived on their own income.

– Although women were – compared to other countries – well educated, they were often educated according to that dual model which assigned men and women different places in the family and within society: even if boys and girls attended the same class, girls had additional lessons in needlework or other so-called female skills instead of mathematics. In this respect Switzerland does not differ so much from other countries. But in the given specifically Swiss situation it led to a kind of vicious circle: teachers and politicians were convinced that Switzerland needed well-educated people because Swiss industry relied on skilled work as a result of the absence of mineral resources. Although Swiss women worked in factories and were highly skilled, their skill in textile techniques was not considered the result of training or education but of their gender role. In addition, women's factory work was more and more deemed problematic and, therefore, even vocational education became a male privilege. On the other hand education was considered so important because of politics, the fact that 'everybody' decided about the general policy to be adopted. Therefore, politicians said that everybody must get a considerable amount of education as a citizen – but 'everybody' was male, while women held a different kind of citizenship and needed less education in this respect – which, of course, was later used to say that they did not have enough knowledge to be enfranchised.

– With some modification this also applied to university education. Although women were admitted to university comparatively early, most students were foreign nationals. Swiss women were a minority. There are many reasons for this, but one important reason in our context is that a university degree did not help women in the labour market: they could study law but could not become lawyers or judges because 'active citizenship' (which meant suffrage) was a precondition.

And in the civil service, they had to leave the job as soon as they married. University education was worth less for women.

Paradoxically – thus my argument – the same political factors which furthered women's political activities and were responsible for the improvement of women's civil rights and which you might expect to lead to political rights delayed the introduction of political equality for women.

3. The Women's Movement and the Struggle for the Vote 1872–1945

There was no direct influence of Julie von May's petition concerning women's rights on the new constitution, but the constitutional change of 1874 nevertheless had its impact on the structure of women's organisations: although most of the federalistic structures of Switzerland and the autonomy of the cantons remained untouched by the constitutional change the power of the federal institutions and the federal government was strengthened, making it necessary for political associations to organise on the federal level.[ ] This held true as well for women's organisations and led to the formation of supra-regional women's associations, of bourgeois as well as of working class character, gaining political influence. The bourgeois organisations like the 'Verein zur Hebung der Sittlichkeit', a descendant of the abolitionist movement and 'Gemeinnützige Frauenverein' were aiming at moral and social reform of society by women.[17] Working women's associations, founded in 1886, and forming a national association in 1890 were connected to the national and international working class movement. Women's political emancipation was part of their programme but did not make specific action necessary as, according to their ideology, the discrimination of women was to be abolished by the realisation of a socialist society.

In the 1890s some women's organisations of a new type were founded in Geneva, Zürich, Berne and Lausanne. They called themselves 'progressive' and were explicitly striving for equal rights: such as access to higher education, equal pay, equal job opportunities. They organised a

---

17 See Brigitte Schnegg, Anne-Marie Stalder, 'Zur Geschichte der schweizerischen Frauenbewegung', in *Die Stellung der Frau in der Schweiz*, published by the Eidgenöss. Frauenkommission, Teil IV: *Frauenpolitik* (Bern: 1984).

congress, 'Kongress für die Interessen der Frau' in 1896, in order to demonstrate the importance of women's achievements in society. Delegates
of all kinds of women's organisations including working women's organisations participated as well as (male) politicians who expressed their
opinion on women's role in public. To further co-operation with the
progressive associations they founded an organisation, the 'Bund Schweizerischer Frauenvereine' (BSF) in 1898.

Whilst this organisation proved incapable of taking decisive steps on
the question of women's suffrage, a number of cantonal associations for
women's suffrage were organising around the turn of the century: Zürich (1896, 1906), Neuchâtel and Olten (1905), Geneva, the Canton of
Vaud (1906). They were united in 1909 in an organisation the 'Schweizerischer Frauenstimmrechtsverein' (Women's Suffrage Movement), but
continued their work as well on the cantonal level. Since Carl Hilty's
article, it had become commonly accepted that it would be easier to
achieve suffrage in the cantons and then apply it to the federal level.

In 1912, another decisive step in matters of women's suffrage was
taken when the Social Democratic Party decided at their congress, to
take up the question wherever possible. As a result social-democratic
politicians began to demand cantonal plebiscites on this issue.[18] The first
cantonal plebiscites took place in Neuchâtel in 1919, and in Basel in
1920. 69 per cent of the male voters in Neuchâtel and 65 per cent of
the male voters in Basel decided against women's suffrage. The very same
day (February 8th 1920), Zürich held a plebiscite, the result was even
worse (80 per cent nays). Geneva was to follow in 1921 with about the
same result as Basel. There were about 25 cantonal plebiscites altogether,
in some cantons like Basel and Geneva it took several attempts before
the male citizenship granted women full political citizenship. In Basel
it took 7, in Geneva 5 attempts before women were successful on the
cantonal level. Before the Second World War seven cantons took up the
issue of women's suffrage – all with distinctly negative results. Both sides
used concepts of equality and difference and referred to the principle
of equality in the constitution. Supporters of women's suffrage argued
that because men and women were equal as human beings, women had

18 Women and their organizations could of course not do this – they were not
members of the parliaments after all.

an innate right to decide on political matters, others argued that because women dealt with political questions differently, because they differ from men, it was at once a matter of justice and of prudence to take their view into consideration. Opponents argued that article 4 of the constitution – 'all Swiss are equal before the law' – did not legitimate – what they called – an 'absolute and mechanistic notion of equality' but allowed, or even demanded, to take existing differences into consideration.[19] For them motherhood represented the profound difference between men and women, establishing a status of dependence not compatible with the notion of a free and independent voter, while for the supporters of female suffrage motherhood was a positive argument: the responsibility of women for children furthered their insight in social affairs, decided at the polls. Neither supporter nor opponents contested the view that political participation of women was a question to be decided by the male citizenship, thus accepting the supremacy of Swiss traditions over a supra-national concept of human rights.[20]

Despite the failure on the cantonal level women's organisations did not give up and took the issue up on the federal level in 1929 by petitioning the federal parliament. The petition was signed by about 250,000 people, mostly women. The government accepted the petition but did not consider any concrete measure.

It was only after the Second World War that the question was taken up for the first time by the Federal Parliament. The first debate on women's suffrage on this level took place in 1945 in the National Council. Apart from the Social Democratic Party all other parties were divided on the question but at the end of the debate the National Council decided for women's suffrage and commissioned the government by a majority of 104 votes to 35 to solve the question and to propose measures of introduction of a constitutional amendment (of course to be approved by the male citizens) and ordered them to report to Parliament. This took them a full 12 years.

This development was only possible because the majority of Swiss men and a considerable number of Swiss women accepted that the

19 Fleiner/Giacometti, *Schweizerisches Bundesstaatsrecht* (Zürich: 1949), p. 406.
20 Only in the 1950s did the Association for Women's Suffrage try to reinterpret the Constitution.

structure of Swiss political measures – especially the plebiscite – was more important than human rights. The political structures – above all a constitution which made (and still makes) even fundamental human rights[21] subject to the consent of the majority of voters and of the cantons – gave them the chance to delay the introduction of suffrage.

The question, however, why Swiss men wanted it this way, and why they feared the political participation of women has only been answered partially by this analysis of rather complicated political structures. There probably is another explanation: like all privileged groups, Swiss men only reluctantly share their rights and give up their privileges. Political participation did not only mean voting, and politics was not only a matter of a few politicians but it was – especially in smaller communities – part of everyday male life. It took a lot of men's leisure time and it was held to confer high status. There were many political decisions to be taken, there were several plebiscites every year, and there were weekly or monthly meetings of commissions and meetings of the community assembly, and there were elections and so on – and there was always the pub afterwards. Politics was part of a male-defined culture, a resort – a haven free of women – and after all men could not imagine women usurping their last retreat, one of the last bastions of male supremacy.

21 This not only holds with political rights, but also with other fundamental rights such as asylum or the naturalisation of foreigners.

At the end of the 19th century, the Swiss political institutions 'Initiative' and 'Referendum', instruments of Swiss direct democracy were adopted by several American states. Ironically, in propaganda cartoons it was a Swiss lady who presented these instruments of direct democracy to an American lady. At that time a Swiss woman had no political rights, but in some of the American states women were already enfranchised. From: James H. Hutson, *The Sister Republics. Die Schweiz und Vereinigten Staaten von 1776 bis heute* (Bern: Stämpfli, 1992: 76).

Motherhood was declared incompatible with political participation as shown in this poster against women's suffrage in the cantonal campaign of the Canton of Basel in 1927.
(Text: 'Mother is meddling in politics')

BRIGITTE STUDER

The Rise of 'Public Woman'

Politics, Citizenship and Gender in the Swiss Debate on Female Suffrage after World War Two

If Switzerland forms a special case in the history of female suffrage, it is not because there was no early debate nor was it due to a lack of a significant suffragist movement.[1] Its singularity lies more in the fact that it was the first European country to grant both active and passive political rights to all its male citizens on a permanent basis in the 19th century, and practically the last to grant these same rights to its female citizens in the 20th century.[2] A second singularity is the way in which female suffrage was introduced since it had to be approved at all the organisational levels of the government by a majority of (male) citizens. Finally, compared with other countries, these political rights are more far-reaching as they include not only the passive and active right of election, but also, since 1874, the right to initiate reform and to hold a referendum. Apart from choosing his or her representatives, the political

---

1   On the beginnings of the history of female suffrage in Switzerland, see Beatrix Mesmer, *Ausgeklammert, eingeklammert. Frauen und Frauenorganisationen in der Schweiz des 19. Jahrhunderts* (Basel: Helbing & Lichtenhahn, 1988), pp. 245–267; Nora Escher, *Entwicklungstendenzen der Frauenbewegung in der deutschen Schweiz 1850–1918/19* (Zürich: ADAG Administration & Druck AG, 1985). Also useful are two books written by participants in the struggle: Lotti Ruckstuhl, *Frauen sprengen Fessel. Hindernislauf zum Frauenstimmrecht in der Schweiz* (Bonstetten: Interfeminas Verlag, 1986); Susanna Woodtli, *Gleichberechtigung. Der Kampf um die politischen Rechte der Frau in der Schweiz* (Frauenfeld: Verlag Huber, 1975). For this contribution I had the opportunity to consult a recent Ph.D. thesis which retraces in detail the long battle for female suffrage as well as the arguments of its defendants and opponents after 1945: Yvonne Voegeli, *Zwischen Hausrat und Rathaus. Auseinandersetzungen um die politische Gleichberechtigung der Frauen in der Schweiz 1945–1971*, Ph.D. Univ. of Zurich, 1994. I am grateful to the author for letting me read her work before publication.

2   Of all European countries only Portugal granted the vote later to all its female citizens.

citizen also makes decisions on a series of political, social, economic and cultural questions relating to the locality, the canton and the Confederation. My supposition is that the Swiss singularity, the time lag of 123 years (if we count on a national level, and 143 years if we take into consideration the last canton to grant women the right to vote in 1991) between the introduction of the male right to vote and that of the female right to vote, can be explained precisely by these two characteristics of the political system. On the one hand, the acquisition of the right to vote by women depended on the agreement of the majority of the male citizens, which gave weight to the voice of the remotest defenders of archaism. On the other hand, compared to other democracies, the right solicited by women was a 'value added' political right. This distinction means that Swiss political rights retained the aura of decisive rights for a longer period of time, even though many members of parliament since the fifties acknowledged that women's right to vote and to eligibility had scarcely modified the political majorities in neighbouring countries.

Moreover, certain contextual factors which, for historiography, favoured the extension of political rights to women in other countries during the first half of the century, did not exist in Switzerland or did not take on the same meaning there. So the Swiss women's movement did not achieve a 'conquest-vote', as it attained neither the magnitude of the moderate American suffragists, nor the radicalism of the English suffragettes.[3] Between 1934 and 1968, the number of members of the Swiss Association for Female Suffrage, founded in 1909, fluctuated between 4–6,000 members and a radical wing was practically non-existent.[4] Moreover, it had to face not just one single obstacle on a national level, but had to clear opposition at all levels and suffered from the

---

3 For these distinctions, see Françoise Thébaud, 'Guerre, civisme et citoyenneté des femmes. Essai d'analyse d'une mutation', in Eliane Viennot (ed.), *La démocratie 'à la française' ou les femmes indésirables* (Paris : Publications de l'Université Paris 7, 1996), pp. 77–83.

4 It had 5,567 members in 1934, 4,133 in 1951, 5,734 in 1955 and about 6,300 in 1968 (Voegeli, *Zwischen Hausrat und Rathaus*, p. 405). The earliest suffrage association was founded in Geneva in 1907. The request for the right to vote was first formulated individually by a feminist named Meta von Salis Marschlins in the 1880s, lawyers started debating the question in the 1890s.

divisions imposed by federalism. Nor could it take advantage, at the end of the First World War, of the 'political-strategy vote' which, according to Richard Evans, was one of the methods used by the Liberals and the Reformists to stabilise democracy and restrain the expansion of Communism in Central Europe, notably in Germany.[5] A third interpretation attributes the acquisition of the right to vote to women's patriotic commitment during the two world wars. This is the theory of the 'reward-vote' put forward by Arthur Marwick.[6] Its value is disputed today by women's history, as it does not explain why certain countries such as Great Britain, a belligerent country, Sweden and Holland, neutral countries, granted women the right to vote, whereas others such as Switzerland or France did not do so. Furthermore, many authors consider that the impact of the war on the social relations between the sexes was basically conservative since it reinforced a polarized vision of feminine and masculine roles.[7] Above all, this interpretation probably confuses the hopes of the feminists and the true motives behind the establishment of the vote for women.

In Switzerland, as elsewhere, the end of each war led the suffragists to believe that from now on a spread of democracy belonged to the realm of the possible. 'The present desire in the world [...] is not just to reconstruct everything, but to improve on many things, especially in the political field' said a Swiss feminist in 1945.[8] The militants for female suffrage based their optimism on their participation in the national effort – economic and charitable in 1914, also military in 1939. They considered that their public-spiritedness should provide the proof of their capacity as citizens. However, they rarely put forward this 'service

5 Richard Evans, *The Feminists. Women's Emancipation Movements in Europe, America and Australia, 1840–1920* (London/New York: Croom Helm/Barnes & Noble Books, 1977).

6 *Women at War, 1914–1918* (Glasgow: Fontana Paperbacks, 1977); *War and Social Change in the Twentieth Century: A Comparative Study of Britain, France, Germany, Russia and the United States* (London: 1979).

7 See for example, Françoise Thébaud, *La femme au temps de la guerre de 14* (Paris: Stock, 1986); Ute Daniel, *Arbeiterfrauen in der Kriegsgesellschaft: Beruf, Familie und Politik im Ersten Weltkrieg* (Göttingen: Vandenhoeck und Ruprecht, 1989).

8 Bila Pesch-Felmeth, *Das Aktivbürgerrecht der Frau. Referat gehalten anlässlich der Versammlung der Genossenschafterinnen des Lebensmittelvereins Zürich am 5. November 1945*, quoted by Voegeli, *Zwischen Hausrat und Rathaus*, p. 40.

rendered to the country in difficult times'[9] as an argument to claim political acknowledgement of their commitment. All this leads one to believe that until the 1950s, or even 1960, the moral codes of Swiss politics, based on duty and self-sacrifice, excluded the call for a particular right. But this modesty, which should have been used to further demonstrate the civil maturity of women, was used, on the contrary, against female suffrage by its adversaries. While the feminists hoped that the acknowledgement of their work and their efforts would quite naturally ensue from 'justice and dignity',[10] their attitude only reinforced the opinion of the politicians that the country owed them nothing and that they were asking for nothing. In the debate in the Houses in December 1945 on the Oprecht postulate in favour of women's right to vote, the Minister Eduard von Steiger expressed his 'esteem' for the suffragists for not drawing attention to 'how much the Swiss population owed to women during the war', which thus allowed parliament 'to freely debate the question'.[11] And to come to the conclusion that the question was not urgent as long as women were not demanding the right to vote!

This outcome clearly illustrates the basic dilemma of the Swiss feminists: if they respected the narrow margins tolerated by the rules of conduct granted by the federal system, their demands could easily be ignored by the politicians. On the other hand, as soon as they ventured beyond these codes of propriety, they were attacked by abusive speeches, written and spoken as well as illustrated. Their conduct was sanctioned by derision, caricature, slander, libel and denunciation.

These limits placed on the political activity of the Swiss suffragists doubtless indicate in part why the right to vote was acquired so late in Switzerland. The absence of the slightest conception, in a context of greater social stability, of political conditions favouring a democratic expansion are yet more elements that explain why the Swiss lagged behind in this domain. These factors, put forward by foreign research

---

9 Association suisse pour le suffrage féminin, *Rapports des sections ayant passé par des votations cantonales dès 1934* ([n.p., n.d]), p. 22.

10 Hortensia Zängerle, *Die öffentlich-rechtliche Stellung der Frau in der Schweiz* (Wil: Buchdruckerei A. Meyerhans, 1940), p. 113.

11 *Amtliches stenographisches Bulletin des Nationalrats/Bulletin sténographique du Conseil national* (Bern 1945), p. 724.

to understand why, in certain countries, the opposition to female suffrage was overcome at such or such a time in the first half of the 20th century, indicate, for Switzerland, the difficulties of the feminists in view of the absence of any such favourable circumstances. Nevertheless, this perspective of factual history leaves aside the primary question of the origin or the reasons for the opposition to female suffrage. What was at stake in women's right to vote? Why did male Swiss citizens stubbornly refuse to share a right that they possessed since 1848 and which was considered to be *the* main characteristic of a democracy? What kind of an understanding of democracy and citizenship did that imply? What image of 'woman' fostered this refusal, what place in society was she granted, how were the gender relations conceptualized in politics?

It is, without doubt, precisely because of its singularity that the Swiss case can prove to be instructive regarding these basic questions of the conception of modern democracy. If we adapt the phrase used by a national councillor during the debate in the Houses in 1958[12] it was in 'the most advanced male democracy' that opposition was the most determined. My hypothesis is that the reason is to be found not so much in a compensatory phenomenon in relation to the early introduction of the male vote, as asserted by Pierre Rosanvallon in connection with France, but in the very principle of this vote.[13] Indeed, to use an expression of Françoise Collin, democracy ratifies the equality of equals. Citizenship is a social construction based on the 'vir' and not on the human being 'homo'.[14] The political or public sphere was, as for example Carole Pateman has shown, considered to be masculine. Women were excluded from it because they do not have the liberty and the independence that defined the citizen.[15] Consequently, to grant them the right to vote amounted to regarding and proclaiming them to be autonomous, to conferring on them a status until then reserved for men. Such a decision was considered to have repercussions which were not limited to the public sphere, since it seemed difficult to reconcile

---

12 *Amtliches stenographisches Bulletin des Nationalrats* (1958), p. 264.
13 *Le sacre du Citoyen* (Paris: Gallimard, 1992), p. 411.
14 'Mythe et réalité de la démocratie', in Viennot (ed.), *La démocratie 'à la française'* *ou les femmes indésirables*, pp. 25–36, here pp. 30 and 32.
15 *The Sexual Contract* (Stanford/Cal.: Stanford University Press, 1988).

granting an independent position to women in their role as citizens while maintaining the wife's dependence in a marriage. Conceding the right to vote to women amounted to first of all questioning the connection between the public and the private sphere, but also renegotiating the relationship between men and women and waiving the rights to male privileges. 'In my opinion, there is only one reason to be against women's right to vote: the fear of losing power', stated a sympathizer to the cause of female suffrage in 1950.[16]

Although it was rare to hear someone speak so frankly, in reality the debates on women's right to vote revolved around the structure of the relations of gender. Also at stake were the definitions of masculinity and femininity. It was only when the respective conceptions of men and women lost their exclusive assimilation to one sphere or the other and that the image of woman as a public person became acceptable that the right to vote would have a chance of being admitted. For this to come about, there had to be preliminary changes in the organisation of the family as well as in public life. The comparative analysis of the debates around the two federal votes of 1959 and 1971 demonstrates this.

Let us specify that these were the only votes on a national level. In spite of numerous parliamentary interventions, the government had always considered that the question was not urgent. If an increasing number of pressures undoubtedly influenced its decision to finally take action in this matter, the direct cause both times lay in other political objectives. In the fifties, the Federal Council wanted to present the people with a mandatory civil defence project which included women; in the following decade, Switzerland, having joined the Council of Europe in 1963, was not in a position to sign the Convention on Human Rights without first introducing a series of legal changes including female suffrage.[17] In spite of similar circumstances, the two debates were very different in nature. When the Federal Houses debated women's right to vote in 1970, there was no longer any doubt about its imminent introduction. All the parliamentary groups claimed to be in favour of it and

16 Grendelmeier, member of the Alliance of Independents, in the commission on revision of the principles of election of the National Council (the Lower House) (minutes of the commission, 22–23 June 1950, p. 22, quoted in Voegeli, *Zwischen Hausrat und Rathaus*, p. 168).
17 See Voegeli, *Zwischen Hausrat und Rathaus*, pp. 81–92, 105–127.

the various speakers each surpassed one another with declarations on its necessity as a prerequisite of simple justice and its value in making the country benefit from the contributions of its female population. The 1958 debate, on the other hand, was a continuation of the discussions that had been going on for almost a century. On all sides, the arguments remained the same, apart from a slight shading due to the times. In 1919 already, the *Neue Zürcher Zeitung* concluded in relation to the deliberations around the motions in favour of the introduction of female suffrage of Herman Greulich and Emil Göttisheim: 'In general, the prevailing debate has taught us that it is hardly more feasible to examine the women's question with new arguments.'[18] Whilst the opponents of female suffrage predicted a detrimental effect on the family and the country if women obtained the right to vote, the sympathizers, on the contrary, looked on it as a way of improving democracy which would also have an effect on the private sphere. In spite of their antagonistic opinions, they all nevertheless shared the same assumption: men and women are creatures of differing natures with specific qualities which determine their respective functions in society: women are responsible for the family, men are made for public life. This vision that women's primary responsibility lies in their duties toward their families united both opponents and defenders of female suffrage. So we can read in the Federal Council's 1957 message on the introduction of female suffrage, which was intended to be a compromise between the two positions: 'Therefore when we hear it said that women belong in the home, it is certainly true, in spite of the liberalisation of the family in the meantime.'[19] In 1970, we find the same line of thought, though with a new accent: the primary attachment of the woman is still the family, but it is no longer considered to be exclusive. 'Women should, as far as is possible, attend to their family duties in the home, according to their vocations and special aptitudes', noted the Federal Council in its message. 'But this commitment has declined and in many cases no longer exists.'[20]

Indeed, the notion of a polarity between male and female was accepted almost unanimously. Only a few individuals dared to contradict this consensus on an ontological gender difference. But the price

18 Nr 850, 26 June 1919
19 *Bundesblatt* vol. I (1957), p. 749.
20 *Bundesblatt* vol. I (1970), p. 82.

to pay for such dissension was high, as the feminist Iris von Roten discovered in 1958 with her book *Women in the Playpen*, in which she vigorously denounced 'the supervised freedom' of women. In a very personal, controversial style, she treated all the theories on the 'female difference' as vulgar wrapping to 'sweeten the inferiority' of women.[21] She triggered an outcry, and even the foremost women's organisation in Switzerland, the Alliance of Female Societies, 'energetically' kept its distance.[22]

Undeniably, Iris von Roten's arguments touched a sensitive point when she attacked the differentialist theories since these formed the foundation of the concepts on the social order of gender, not only of the opponents to female suffrage, but also of its advocates. Nevertheless a dissension was apparent with regard to the interpretation of this difference, more complementary or more egalitarian. In the second case, women's responsibility to the family did not exclude their commitment in the public sphere.[23] But neither would the right to vote 'prevent women from remaining at the heart of the family, the keeper of the home, the one who watches over the unit that is indispensable as the mainstay of society'.[24] The suffragists did not by any means wish 'to snatch women from the home'.[25]

---

21 *Frauen im Laufgitter. Offene Worte zur Stellung der Frau* (Berne: Verlag Hallwag, 1958). She also wrote a sarcastic guide to the women's vote, *Frauenstimmrechtsbrevier. Vom schweizerischen Patentmittel gegen das Frauenstimmrecht, den Mitteln gegen das Patentmittel, und wie es mit oder ohne doch noch kommt* (Basle: Frobenius Verlag, 1959).

22 On this campaign, see Yvonne-Denise Köchli, *Eine Frau kommt zu früh. Das Leben der Iris von Roten, Autorin von «Frauen im Laufgitter»* (Zurich: Weltwoche-ABC Verlag, 1992), pp. 101–118.

23 See, for instance, ... *im Sinne der Gerechtigkeit in der Demokratie ... Orientierung über die Einführung des Frauenstimm- u. Wahlrechts in eidgenössischen Angelegenheiten*, ed. by Arbeitsgemeinschaft der schweizerischen Frauenverbände für die politischen Rechte der Frau (Berne: 1958), pp. 38–39.

24 The deputy from the canton of Fribourg, Gustave Roulin (Christian Democrat), in favour of female suffrage, in the Upper House, 23 September 1970 (*Amtliches stenographisches Bulletin des Ständerats*, 1970, p. 275). Similarly, another defendant of the vote, the representative from Ticino Alberto Verda (Catholic Conservative) declared: 'Ripeto che la famiglia e la casa restano la base delle aspirazioni della donna nel nostro paese.' (*Amtliches stenographisches Bulletin des Nationalrats*, 1958, p. 275).

This was exactly what the antisuffragists did not believe. For them, the introduction of the female vote meant encouraging an evolution that was already harmful, which had begun with women's paid work and been accelerated by the government taking responsibility for more and more educational and social duties and by industry proposing goods previously produced at home. Rather than favouring this tendency to equality, they preferred to maintain the complementarity between the social functions of man and woman and to guarantee the separation between private and public life, family and politics. Family life had to be protected from politics. If the latter were to intrude on the family, it would only stir up trouble, was the opinion, for example, of the Member of Parliament Werner Christen in 1958.[26] Using different words, the spokesman for the group opposed to female suffrage which formed a vocal minority within the National Council's committee said more or less the same thing: the fact that women did not have the vote was a welcome correction to the over-politicizing of modern life.[27]

The antisuffragists felt that the family unit was threatened by individualism, which would gain yet more ground if women were granted the right to vote. In 1958, to mitigate this so-called danger, the State Councillor from Aargau, Xaver Stöckli, a Catholic Conservative, again extracted from the filing cabinet, a proposition dear to his party: the family vote.[28] To grant one vote per family was, in his opinion, even more justifiable since the Federal Council declared in its message that 90% of women would vote the same as men. 'Is it not enough then to have one single vote as the family vote, do we not also obtain with that up to 90% of the same result' he asked without worrying that the 10%

25 The representative from the canton of Lucerne, Karl Wick (Catholic Conservative), opposed to the vote, in the Lower House, 19 March 1958 (*Amtliches stenographisches Bulletin des Nationalrats*, 1958, p. 264).

26 *Amtliches stenographisches Bulletin des Ständerats* (1958), p. 400; Christen was a Catholic Conservative from the canton of Nidwald.

27 Karl Wick in the Lower House (*Amtliches stenographisches Bulletin des Nationalrats*, 1958, p. 264).

28 The theorician of Swiss conservatism, Carl Doka, had made a similar proposal in 1934, with the only difference that the head of family would have obtained a double vote (*Verfassungsreform. Die ersten zusammenfassenden Vorschläge für eine neue Bundesverfassung auf konservativer Grundlage* (Einsiedeln: 1934), pp. 67–68).

whose opinions differed would not have a say in the matter.[29] Without
going quite so far, many opponents to the female vote also agreed that
women were more than adequately represented by their husbands. Some
even positively embraced Rousseau's idea that women had a strong influence on men, underestimated but very effective, which had led to
the achievement of a Swiss legislation favourable to women, in spite of
the absence of the right to vote. A female opponent observed in the
Neue Zürcher Zeitung that women owed this indirect influence 'to their
feminine authority and actions and not to a political design'.[30]

Similarly, the opponents discerned in the female vote an adaptation
of women to men, to the detriment of feminine behaviour. They considered that women, as such, would suffer from it. According to Karl
Wick in the National Council, they would risk 'being degraded into a
second class man'.[31] It would be much more beneficial for women and
for the country if they were to concentrate on their own capabilities
and devote themselves entirely to the family and the home and the
education of the next generation. However, in these domains, a certain
expansion of their activities towards the public sphere seemed acceptable. They could be active in school or parish committees, welfare or
tutelage, but in no way should they 'lower themselves' by going into
politics. 'As far as I am concerned, there is always something unfemi-
nine about a woman who climbs into the political arena' declared the
future Minister Rudolf Gnägi, whose Party of Farmers, Independents
and Craftsmen was the stronghold against female suffrage in the National
Council in 1958.[32]

But why were politics and femininity seen as incompatible? It will
be easier to understand the archaic ideas at stake if we consider for a
moment the statements of the people's representatives from a canton
which maintained the tradition of the Landsgemeinde. Resistance there
was the longest and the most persistent. During the 1958 debate, all the
speakers from these cantons were violently opposed to the introduction
of female suffrage. The principle of the Landsgemeinde is that all the

29 *Amtliches stenographisches Bulletin des Ständerats* (1958), p. 393.
30 Verena Keller, 'Die Gründe gegen das Frauenstimmrecht in der Schweiz', *Neue
   Zürcher Zeitung*, Nr 212, 24 January 1959.
31 *Amtliches stenographisches Bulletin des Nationalrats* (1958), p. 266.
32 ibid., p. 270.

citizens participate. But this would not be possible with female suffrage, as someone had to look after house and home, stated the Catholic Conservative from Nidwald, Joseph Odermatt, in 1958.[33] Therefore, in order to work, the Landsgemeinde had to remain a male bastion.

The presence of women at this institution first of all disturbed its progress, but more generally, women's participation in the exercise of democracy set in motion the whole symbolism of the gender order. Karl Wick explained: 'One is never a human being as such, but always a man or a woman.'[34] With female suffrage, women would be delegates to a party, whereas at present they were appointed to a commission as women, to represent the female world, reiterated Karl Hackhofer, the Catholic from Zurich.[35] Women would become more masculine, men would weaken, and women would be the first to regret the situation since they would no longer have someone whom they could look up to, predicted a newspaper of the Zurich Women's Alliance against Female Suffrage in 1966.[36] Moreover, the breaking down of barriers between family and politics would create direct rivalry between men and women. Women would be the main victims since they would lose the protection to which they had had a right until then, and they were the weaker of the two. 'Full equal rights between men and women means legally committing complete political and economic rivalry between men and women, and only increases the tension between men and women to the detriment of the latter', declared the aforementioned Karl Wick.[37] Finally, the opponents to female suffrage saw in it extra responsibilities for women since, according to their vision of the social organisation of gender, with political activity they would have access to another sphere of society and their duties would be added to the tasks which were already their responsibility. 'Because we respect women and in many ways hold them in higher esteem than ourselves, so we wish to quite simply protect them from the new cares that arise from the

33 ibid., p. 279.
34 ibid., p. 264.
35 ibid., p. 285.
36 *Der Züri-Bote*, ed. by the Bund der Zürcherinnen gegen das Frauenstimmrecht (Zurich: 1966).
37 Karl Wick in the Lower House (*Amtliches stenographisches Bulletin des Nationalrats*, 1958, p. 265).

entitlement and duty to vote', said Werner Meister from Berne, another member of the Party of Farmers, Independents and Craftsmen, to the Houses in 1958.[38]

In the opposite camp, the sympathizers of female suffrage endeavoured to convince their opponents that its introduction would not modify the gender order, but on the contrary, would enrich both politics and society. To begin with, there was the message from the Federal Council in February 1957 which adopted this strategic argument of the women's movement.[39] Here we read that: 'It is to be expected that women in all fields, for which they possess special qualities and inclinations, will give fresh impetus and stimulation to political life, and this should not be renounced, whatever the price.'[40] From the 'female mentality' one wished for a 'new accent in politics'.[41] Some even awarded the task of regenerating democracy to women. 'Let us hope that the participation of the female electoral body will stimulate the male voter to return to the polls', remarked the Conservative from Fribourg, Jean Bourgknecht, in 1958.[42] According to its defenders, the introduction of the female vote should also have beneficial effects on the family and women's related duties, particularly on the quality of the education of its future citizens.[43]

---

38 *Amtliches stenographisches Bulletin des Nationalrats* (1958), p. 281.
39 On the notion of 'Republican motherhood', designed to bring the motherly qualities of women into society, see Paula Baker, 'The Domestication of Politics. Women and American Political Society, 1780–1920', in: *The American Historical Review* 89, 3 (1984), pp. 620–647. For the use made of this idea by the Swiss women's movement, see, for example, *Staatsbürgerin*, Nr 7/8, July/Aug. 1946, p. 3; Hilde Vérène Borsinger, *Die kulturelle Bedeutung der Schweizerin in Familie und Vaterland* (St. Gallen: F. Schwald Druckerei, 1946), p. 18.
40 *Bundesblatt*, I (1957), p. 750.
41 Walo von Greyerz, from Berne and member of the Radical Party (the Liberals), in the Lower House in 1958 (*Amtliches stenographisches Bulletin des Nationalrats*, 1958, p. 276). He was the only representative of his party to participate in the debate. He was in favour of female suffrage.
42 *Amtliches stenographisches Bulletin des Ständerats* (1958), p. 401.
43 See, for example, Schweizerischer Verband für das Frauenstimmrecht, *Das Frauenstimmrecht in der Schweiz. Tatsachen und Auskünfte* ([n.p.], 1950), p. 33. Or the intervention of the Social Christian from Zürich Adelrich Schuler in the Lower House in 1958 (*Amtliches stenographisches Bulletin des Nationalrats*, 1958, p. 291).

The sympathizers of women's right to vote also attempted to break down the resistance to change by demonstrating how the line separating private and public life had, in reality, been overrun by socio-economic changes. The family was no longer a self-sufficient entity, but a consumer group closely dependent on the market economy, stated the Berne Catholic, Jean Gressot, in the National Council.[44] And it was precisely women who linked the two together. On the other hand, the modern State which was no longer just a State of order and police, but also a Welfare State, regularly intervened in many ways in the family through the services it provided.[45] Women therefore already belonged to a large extent to the public sphere, the right to vote would basically not change anything, it was argued.

They also endeavoured to allay the opponents' fears that they would be placed in a minority position by a majority of female voters. With this in mind, the Federal Council's message before the first national vote drew on the lessons learnt from foreign experiences: generally, women were divided amongst themselves politically, their participation at the polls was lower than that of men, and they often gave their preference to male candidates. From all this, the government reached the conclusion: 'We must acknowledge from these facts that political leadership clearly remains with men, and that women's right to vote has in no way resulted in a political influence equal to man's.'[46] Women, it was stated, also made less use of their active citizenship, and were less often candidates on the electoral lists. In this regard, Walo von Greyerz was anxious to reassure his colleagues in the National Council: 'Following their natural leanings, women will continue to leave the greater part of politics to men [...] So we do not need to fear that with one blow, half of this room will become female.'[47] These arguments minimising the influence of the female vote undeniably had more effect on the reticences of the antisuffragists than demands for justice and human rights. For, as far as the opponents were concerned, they had no doubt that 'By granting political rights to women [...] not only will

---

44 *Amtliches stenographisches Bulletin des Nationalrats* (1958), p. 289.
45 ibid.
46 *Bundesblatt*, I (1957), p. 755.
47 *Amtliches stenographisches Bulletin des Nationalrats* (1958), p. 276.

the family union as such be disturbed, but also, in particular, the proper balance between men and women.'[48]

Faced with this kind of apprehension which saw the whole social structure – and with it their masculine privileges – in danger with the introduction of female suffrage, the question arises why it was finally accepted in 1971 by a majority of male citizens. Although we must bear in mind the desire to obliterate Switzerland's negative image vis-à-vis the international community, this aspect is, however, quite relative as it concerns, above all, the federal authorities, and to a lesser extent the population. Moreover, in 1959 already, Switzerland was the last democratic country in Europe to refuse this right to women. If we analyse the debates in the Houses and the voting campaign in the press, three factors emerge. Firstly, we notice the significance acquired by concepts such as 'justice' and 'human rights', which had remained widely absent in the former debates. Switzerland's membership of the Council of Europe doubtless had something to do with it, but it can also be explained by the fact that the women's movement was no longer afraid of quite naturally using these ideas and claiming rights, whereas in the fifties, it had tended to justify itself by arguing that the vote would allow women to better accomplish their family duties and that society as a whole would benefit from women's civic commitment.[49] Even more so when, under the pressure of the second feminist wave, new forms of political activity appeared, which were much more aggressive.

Secondly, the right to vote had evidently lost much of its symbolic meaning. On a medium or long term basis, this is demonstrated by the drop in participation.[50] Also, semi-direct democracy was facing competition in the new forms of democracy, short-lived, but increasing at the end of the sixties, such as joint management by wage-earners, union participation, plenary meetings held by the users of service industries. This proliferation of so-called democracy from below in all sectors of social life provoked the Radical from Vaud, Jean-Jacques

48 *Amtliches stenographisches Bulletin des Ständerats* (1951), pp. 375–379.

49 See, for example, Helene Thalmann-Antenen, *Hat die Schweizerfrau eine politische Mission?* (Berne: Buchdruckerei Fritz Pochon-Jent, 1943), p. 24.

50 Peter Gilg, Peter Hablützel, 'Beschleunigter Wandel und neue Krisen (seit 1945)', in: *Geschichte der Schweiz und der Schweizer*, vol. III (Basel: Helbing & Lichtenhahn, 1983), p. 281.

Cevey, chairman of the National Council's committee on the suffrage question, to say: 'How [...] can one maintain today in all fairness that a female employee has no right to speak out on the subject of working conditions, that questions on price and supplies do not concern the housewife, that a mother must not interfere in school affairs.'[51] If, throughout the century, feminists had counted on the vote to obtain radical improvements in other domains, this was no longer the motive for their demand.

Finally, and above all, it seems that the socio-economic changes set in motion by the thirty years of economic boom, in particular women's rise in economic activity and their greater liberty in the public sphere, were beginning to make an impression on the various mentalities.[52] Indeed, it is striking how all the speakers in the Houses in 1970 pleaded the cause of female emancipation. Not that the differentialist vision had been abandoned. The Minister Ludwig von Moos could not have been more explicit: granting the vote meant 'using' for the 'benefit of the country, the public good and politics' women's 'maternal feelings'.[53] If there were changes in the gender relations, they preceded the right to vote, which in no way endangered the family. On the contrary, the vote became a useful tool in helping the authorities to recover a democratic legitimacy undermined at the beginning of the seventies.

To conclude, I hope to have shown some of the mechanisms of the Swiss singularity in the history of women's right to vote, the paradox of the enormous gap in time between the early introduction of male suffrage and the delay before female suffrage was admitted. In my opinion, the reasons can be found in the combination of three factors. The first and principal one arises from the very nature of citizenship as it was conceived in the last century. Direct or semi-direct democracy, in which representation is even more abstract than in parliamentary democracy,

---

51 *Amtliches stenographisches Bulletin des Nationalrats* (1970), p. 444.
52 A preliminary sign of this imminent change was the fact that in 1958 the Swiss Organisation of Catholic women, up to then opposed to the vote, declared itself in favour of it (Simone Prodolliet, *Die katholische Schweizerin und der schwarze Punkt auf der Landkarte Europas. Das katholische Frauenbild im Spiegel der Frauenstimmrechtsdiskussion 1900–1971*, Univ. of Berne 1984, pp. 62–63 (unpublished seminar paper)).
53 *Amtliches stenographisches Bulletin des Nationalrats* (1970), p. 452.

was based on a polarity between women and men, the corollary of which was segregation between the private and public spheres. Man, or more precisely, the father of the family, represented his wife and his children whose interests he defended. With the socio-economic changes of the end of the 19th century, this relationship between civic capacity and family hierarchy had ever since been declining, particularly in countries where the political institutions were centralised and the citizens' right to decide was limited to the election of their representatives. However, in Switzerland, not only are democratic methods more direct than in other countries, but the political system grants more extensive civic prerogatives. This second factor, institutional, favours a certain immobility – or perpetuation of tradition – because of the precedence given to rural, archaic elements of society, but also because of the greater decision-making value attached to the right to vote. Finally, the third factor, the great political events of the 20th century touched Switzerland only indirectly and the country was not affected by sudden changes in the political majority. Periods of regaining power by the ruling party or of establishing national cohesion through institutional revival, which are favourable to creating opportunities to attract new voters (or in the event, female voters), did not exist in Switzerland. To the detriment of women, to whom access to citizenship was not a priority for some and even felt to be a threat by others. As a Swiss Member of Parliament said before the granting of the vote: 'L'Etat, c'est l'homme'.[54] This it remained until 1971.

---

54 Charles Primborgne from Geneva, Catholic Conservative, in favour of female suffrage (*Amtliches stenographisches Bulletin des Nationalrats*, 1958), p. 260.

BEATRICE VON MATT

New Women's Writing in German-speaking Switzerland

The 1970s were a women's decade, and this is also true of Swiss literature. New voices made themselves heard. The attention of women writers was directed towards their own patterns of living and to the language required for these. The overdue women's suffrage of 1971 certainly did not start women writing in Switzerland, but rather its introduction was itself the expression of a time which was more propitious for women. Of course, if women's suffrage had been rejected then once more, anger and a sense of deprivation would have weighed heavily. So the introduction of female suffrage may after all have contributed atmospherically to the increased impetus.

The real impulse came from the women's movement in the USA, in France and Germany. French women theoreticians such as Julia Kristeva, Hélène Cixous and Luce Irigaray were demanding a new status and position for women. German women literature specialists took up their ideas, applied them and provided illustrations of them from texts by German women writers. Writers from Switzerland were, however, often overlooked. For example, Sigrid Weigel, in her book *Die Stimme der Medusa. Schreibweisen in der Gegenwartsliteratur von Frauen* (*The Voice of Medusa. Ways of Writing in Contemporary Women's Literature*), only mentions one writer from Switzerland: Rahel Hutmacher. It is true that the feminist text *par excellence*, *Häutungen* (*Sheddings*) by Verena Stefan, is there, but this writer from Bern then living in Germany was not read as a Swiss woman. Thus women writers from German-speaking Switzerland were at that time more isolated from the wider literary scene than their male colleagues.

The task before me today is to chart women's writing in Germanspeaking Switzerland. To do this, I should like to select and listen to individual exemplary voices. Allow me first of all to draw up a short list.

First Works

The following writers published their first works in the 1970s and 1980s: Erica Pedretti (*Harmloses bitte,* 1970), Margrit Baur (*Von Strassen, Plätzen und ferneren Umständen,* 1971), Gertrud Leutenegger (*Vorabend,* 1975), Verena Stefan (*Häutungen,* 1975), Maja Beutler (*Flissingen fehlt auf der Karte,* 1976), Laure Wyss (*Frauen erzählen ihr Leben. 14 Protokolle,* 1976), Margrit Schriber (*Aussicht gerahmt,* 1976), Claudia Storz (*Jessica mit Konstruktionsfehlern,* 1977), Hanna Johansen (*Die stehende Uhr,* 1978), Eveline Hasler (*Anna Göldin. Letzte Hexe,* 1982), Adelheid Duvanel (*Windgeschichten,* 1980), Hedi Wyss (*Keine Hand frei,* 1980), Rahel Hutmacher (*Wettergarten,* 1980), Verena Stössinger (*Nina. Bilder einer Veränderung,* 1980), Mariella Mehr (*Steinzeit,* 1981). The list could be continued with writers from French-speaking Switzerland or from the Ticino. For example, Anne Cuneo published in 1969 an important women's book, *Mortelle maladie,* followed by *Poussière du réveil,* 1972. Originally Anne Cuneo came from Italy and was then living in Lausanne, where she published her first books. In 1970, Monique Laederach first appeared on the literary scene. Anna Felder, born in Lugano, writes in German and Italian. In 1970 she published her first book *Quasi Heimweh.* Alice Ceresa had already became known in 1967 with *La figlia prodiga* (*The prodigal daughter*).

The 1970s, the 1980s, the 1990s

For reasons of time, however, I must confine myself to a few powerful literary texts from German-speaking Switzerland. A rough categorisation permits individual periods to be distinguished from one another, but I shall not keep strictly to a chronological sequence. In the 1970s, in addition to the documentary transcripts of women's experience, books in the first person are conspicuous, that is to say, those books by women which are seeking and taking tentative steps towards an individual female place of their own and towards a language of their own, and this quest is often a theme of their writing. In the 1980s, there is a more confident tone. Such determined authors as Helen Meier, Adelheid Duvanel or Isolde Schaad make themselves heard. If one looks at the 1990s, which are already half over, quite new ways of writing can be discerned. A generation of daughters, born in the 1960s, is arriving, insolent, often witty, and self-absorbed in a rather more laid-back manner than their mothers: Milena Moser, Andrea Simmen, Nicole Müller, Ruth Schweikert.

Positions must first of all be created before it is possible to distance oneself ironically or polemically from them. A position of belief must be binding, perhaps even have become somewhat ideological, before it can be rejected. So in the 1970s the struggle was still going on. Women were seeking to establish their own form of expression for a world of their own. But even this had been world was still unknown, it was to look different from the one to which they assigned. What is striking is that these exploratory forays create a discourse which is open and unsecured, a truly literary discourse. The uncertainty, the cracks between frequently imprecise intentions and reality, the male patriarchal structures which were only now being more clearly perceived, this gulf promoted at the time a personal discourse which, in literary terms, still holds good today. The first publications of that generation which started out – the books of Pedretti, Baur, Beutler, Leutenegger, Schriber – are perhaps the most exciting and finest in the work of these writers. An untethered inward structure, the aesthetics of incoherence and of broken forms imparts a convincing authenticity to these texts. Each of these books meant a winning of territory, opened up areas of the soul for which stood a style of writing beyond concepts and beyond what is fixed. It was not programmatic literature with mnemonics and instructions. Literature like that dates quickly.

'Vorabend' by Gertrud Leutenegger: A Different Way of Thinking

On a re-reading, *Vorabend* by Gertrud Leutenegger proves to have been a happy chance. Let us take a look at this book of 1975 which in Switzerland caused scarcely less excitement than *Häutungen*, the programmatic feminist text which appeared in the same year. Changes in perspective, the introduction of associations, memories and dreams create an emotional and psychological sphere before which the actual named location, the streets of Zürich between the Niederdorf and the Bahnhofstrasse, recedes. On the eve of a demonstration, the feminine first person figure wishes to try out for herself alone that participation which is required of her. Constant deviation is not only part of the aesthetic mode, losing oneself in confusion signifies also another attitude, a contrary position to the demonstration with its clearly defined signs and slogans. One senses right away that the individual self will not find its place in this organised collective. At the close – after 207 pages – the text reads: 'A short precise moment of open dreaming and they threaten to betray you, overtake you, wall you in between streets which no longer have a way out, madness a shout writhes within you, in the middle of the advancing throng you beat an area free round about you'.

The areas which the individual clears for herself correspond to another way of thinking. Expeditions into memory are part of this, back into childhood and youth, back to past dreams: 'For a long time, I kept tumbling unexpectedly into this dream during the day. Then I was quite strong, quite radiant, quite absent'. The former girl friend Ce, who 'thinks of nothing' and who is fully here as a living entity, incorporates this other mode of being. The memory of her gives the first person narrator 'this easy awareness' of self. The first person narrator becomes aware that she is a girl only because of Ce. Ce expresses herself frequently in unstructured speeches; it sounds not only like a poetic programme, but also like one for everyday living. It makes the self capable of action, of arranging a territory and an order of her own. The flat in the derelict building opposite the Zürich Stock Exchange implies just such a personal world; there, a 'roof landscape without laws' has arisen with marrow plants and meadow flowers on the unsafe balconies.

Nonetheless, a cry cuts through the rebellious idyll, the cry for a 'prayer to madness'. The cry becomes a signal. From this point on in the text, in accordance with an inner logic, mad people appear, mainly women. The reader is given an insight into the psychiatric clinic of 'Burghölzli'. Madness stands for 'wild, uncontrolled life' which would like to let off steam. Lieschen, for example, aged fifty, in her bath: 'She splashed about in the water ... everything swayed, she laughed with a deep gurgling noise, wildly soaped her hair, she stood there, a volcano, a real Marat, a revolution in the bathtub'. That is the watchword: madness as a revolution of genuine, untamed life. Sin, on the other hand, is represented by the pills which deaden this life – that is regulated, everyday behaviour.

Pictures of mad people go through the whole book. Mad people beckon into dreams, and when somebody swims out into the sea, mad women watch from the beach. Such scenes are cut in abruptly, in the process, syntax is simply bypassed or disintegrates completely. That is also a feature of this kind of writing: undermining a sentence structure which follows rules. Adorno, one of the spiritual fathers of this decade, called 'correct writing', 'coherent, aestheticising speaking', an obscenity. An obscenity which runs counter to the new awareness. And the new awareness saw itself as a feminine awareness as well. This is important.

Parallel to Theory

The many-layered and abruptly shifting discourse in *Vorabend* actually takes up on a poetic level all the themes which the French analysts and linguisticians such as Luce Irigaray and Hélène Cixous developed in those years. Irigaray in *Spéculum de l'autre femme* (1974) (Mirror of the other sex) or Cixous in *La veuve et l'écriture* (1977). According to these texts, feminist literary discourse did not follow a prescribed direction, it circled and fluctuated.

Feminist desire corresponds to this speaking and writing. This goes back to phases of life which are dreamlike, pre-conscious (i.e. 'semiotic', according to Kristeva), and so pre-Oedipal. The eroticism which permeates the atmosphere of *Vorabend* displays precisely such traits: an aimless, floating longing moves the first-person figure at one point towards her girl friend Ce, at another point to her young boy friend Te. She does not commit herself to a sexual identity. The self experiences itself in the abolition of lines of demarcation. With *Vorabend*, Gertrud Leutenegger has created a text which is not committed to a programmatic 'écriture féminine', but in fact invents such an 'écriture'. That constituted a poetic revolution – especially in the literature of German-speaking Switzerland.

Divided Consciousness

Permit me to touch now on some other deconstructions of the male,
i.e. the generally recognised place, from the 1970s: In *Mortelle maladie*
of 1969, Anne Cuneo employs quite differing modes of speaking, lyri-
cal, reporting, narrating, to home in on and to name the experience of
birth, motherhood and contact with others, frequently single mothers.
Female experience is seeking a language of its own here too, a language
which sounds like this: 'I must find the strength to survive, beneath the
eyes of my misfortune, beside the blossomleaves of the meat-eating
plants, in the shadow of Annunziata' (from the German version of the
book which appeared in 1975 as *Things covered with Shadows*, translated
by Pierre Imhasly). With Anne Cuneo, too, the position is not fixed –
it is conjured up in a motto with the words of F. Scott Fitzgerald: 'You
have come into a ghostly country that is no longer Here and not yet
There'.

'Here' and 'There': this is the manner in which two incompatible
areas of life are designated in Erica Pedretti's miniatures which have the
title *Harmloses bitte*. 'Here' is the intact snow-shimmering present in the
Engadine, 'there' is the dark region of memory, it is the overgrown summer gardens of the child in Moravia, the approaching war. There is no
abode in which 'Here' and 'There' are contained together.

Maja Beutler, in her first novel *Fuss fassen*, also introduces a consciousness divided in this way. The voice of reason, of abstraction, of ordinari-
ness is, in brief sentences with the title 'Objective', interspersed into
hesitant portrayals of uncertainty and fear. With Maja Beutler, too, her
own truth confronts the habitual.

Certainly, this new perception of writing, as it arose and developed
in Switzerland in the 1970s, also has its dangerous side. The place of
escape attracts *kitsch*. However, if an alert strategy for the text and the
courage to follow the movement of one's own language correspond to
the (women's) questions and the demands for an authentic life, then new
areas full of adventure open themselves to literature. Leutenegger, Pedretti, Cuneo, Schriber, Beutler and Margrit Baur discovered such ter-
ritories twenty years ago.

The Silent Angel of History

From a purely thematic point of view, the journey into the unknown certainly does not always lead to a goal. The other place may beckon temptingly, another way of looking at things, a feminine one, one which would be determined by emotion, momentary fulfilment or giving shape to one's life – but the entry to it can be blocked, it can be behind glass. Margrit Schriber – born in 1939 – has often made the main figures of her books women whose biographies have no prospects, for example, in the first-person narrative *Aussicht gerahmt,* and especially convincingly in the novel *Muschelgarten* of 1984. To the heroine of this latter novel – the woman who loses her reason as the victim of loss of speech – the image of Medusa whom horror gradually causes to fall silent could be applied. This is a myth which at that time was frequently to be found in the writings of Hélène Cixous and Sigrid Weigel – Medusa as the 'silent angel of history' in analogy to Walter Benjamin's 'angel of history'. The lack of future, the state of being struck dumb, has to do with a powerful past, the patriarchal past. The lack of place, the deterritorialisation, is certainly recognised with fear – but language sticks in women's throats. Margrit Schriber has given shape to this fear in *Muschelgarten*. The shell garden is the last possibility of retreat for a sensitive, gifted woman who fails in the world of efficiency and money-making, who chokes slowly in on herself. The woman starts to wander in ever-decreasing circles until she comes to a stop, and she remains at a stop, draped in extravagant pieces of cloth. She makes herself into a doll, a tailor's dummy to some degree – for tailoring, the creative manipulation of materials, would actually have been her preferred work, her art. In the following passage, which I am going to read to you, there is an alternation between the external and the internal perspectives, the woman, 'Arnold's wife', is seen sometimes from outside, sometimes as a first person narrator from within. The constant alternation indicates the sense of being lost, of having no standpoint:

> She is looking at me. She opens and shuts her bushy eyelashes. She turns her head and looks sideways. The dull lips attempt a smile.
> And Arnold's wife is supposed to be missing. On the path lined with shells which runs from the hilltop to the copper beech tree to the pond, she must have got lost between these three points. Disappeared in the Bermuda triangle of Anna's garden.

The brothers and sisters have given up the search, say the customers in *The Lion Inn*. They say that the bushes are getting thicker and thicker. They say that the hedge is growing and the gate is getting rusty. They say that the landlady must be given up for lost.

Arnold should see me like this. As a life-size doll. How beautiful you are! And so young! I open and shut my eyes. I trot along beside him to the furniture department. He undresses me and lays me on the patterned bed. He says I want to give you pleasure and lays himself on top of me. I whimper, I open and close my eyes. Arnold has given me pleasure.

Extreme Desolation

Figures like that, twisted as if by tetanus, are placed by the Basel writer Adelheid Duvanel at the centre of her short stories, starting with *Windgeschichten* of 1980 and continuing until *Die Brieffreundin* in 1995. Mostly, they are women or children. In the volume *Anna und ich* of 1985, the technique has been developed to the point of mastery, and even the simplest texts turn out to be precariously undermined structures. People hang in them. They have no place in society, and are usually hemmed in by such appalling desolation that they seize up, reject all change and do not even suffer any more from their condition. Their imagination distorts the unpropitious circumstances – and themselves at the same time – into grotesque images; they imagine they are shrinking or sticking to the wall. Almost autistically, they become from time to time monsters who accept only their own distorted view of the world. This is probably the most extreme form of rejection, of withdrawal into the self, that it is possible to imagine.

In comparison, the saddest stories by women, as for example the transcripts recorded by the Zürich writer Laure Wyss (born 1913) under the title *Frauen erzählen ihr Leben* (*Women recount their lives*), still manage somehow to sound hopeful – and even if only on account of the carefree vital language of the reports, not infrequently a mixture of High German and dialect. The presentation of such 'authentic' reports was a typical feature of the 1970s; documentary collections such as those of Laure Wyss were also to be found in the Federal Republic of Germany and in the German Democratic Republic. Having women recount their often unspectacular lives was an obvious way of conducting a 'recherche féminine'.

Reflection in History and Myth

Another procedure is to create a reflection against history or myth. A specific contemporary life and development are considered against the reflection of an earlier one, frequently of a historically well-known biography. In this respect, another example from Laure Wyss could be mentioned, namely *Weggehen ehe das Meer zufriert*; contemporary events are interwoven with those of the rebellious Queen Christine of Sweden, who abdicates after ruling for ten years, converts to Catholicism, moves to Rome and can assert at the end of her life: 'I was born free, I live free and I will die liberated'.

Eveline Hasler works in a similar fashion, for example in *Anna Göldin. Letzte Hexe* (1982) or in the novel *Die Wachsflügelfrau. Geschichte der Emily Kempin-Spyri* (1991). Erica Pedretti, in *Valerie oder Das unerzogene Auge*, goes back to a model of a specific kind, to Valentine Godé-Darel, whom the painter Ferdinand Hodler recorded in countless drawings as she lay dying. This was the only way Hodler could approach his beloved mistress, by distancing her from himself in his work. In 1985, Pedretti wrote a similar story. Valerie is suffering from cancer; on her sickbed, she is drawn by Franz, her lover. He takes her as his model, divides her up into proportions and lines and maintains an external view in so doing. Valerie becomes keenly alert as a result of her illness, she learns to live a new rich life. She gives herself up to dreams, surrenders to images and half-images, writes them down. And this is how the language of this book reads; with intuitive calculation, it reproduces the anarchic play of the imagination. A humming, vibrating corpus of language is created, and becomes the poetic document of an other, of a feminine life – albeit against the background of death. Two systems of notation, that of the man and that of the woman, become entangled. The disintegration of the male system also succeeds mimetically, that is to say, in language and with language. The structures are not only explicitly called in question from outside, but also from the interior of the sentences and the words. Thus a new manner of speaking is born, in a similar fashion to Leutenegger's *Vorabend*. The reflection of the narrator in Valentine Godé-Darel imparts something like validity and historical depth to the book; it banishes the chance elements which can remain with a single isolated story told only once.

A Bolder Approach: Helen Meier

The books of Helen Meier in the 1980s look like the complete opposite to those just discussed. No less rich artistically, they are structured
differently, are bold in approach, hard, analysing. This writer, who displays a wildly defiant attitude to language, first appeared on the literary scene at the age of fifty-five at the competition in Klagenfurt for
the Ingeborg Bachmann Literary Prize. Since then, Helen Meier has
been a powerful presence. She stakes out a contrary position to subtle
seekers like Leutenegger or Pedretti, Margrit Baur or Maja Beutler.
Helen Meier harbours scarcely any illusions about a more equitable
distribution of the roles of the sexes. Coolly, she records futilities and
cracks everywhere in society, and also between men and women. But
this occurs with such vital self-confidence that each of her books also
expresses the happiness engendered by artistic sovereignty, by the tri-
umph of writing over the world as it is. Thus writing has for the autobiographical figure of Anna in the novel *Lebenleben* (1989) an almost
ritual origin, and has an inner link with childhood and with the forgotten religion of that early period. Happiness means letting the soul
become word.

Helen Meier's protagonists draw their autonomy and strength from
lonely rebellion, from the revolt against men, a revolt which they conduct alone. In the stories in the collection *Das Haus am See*, which all
have a house at their centre, the 'experiment of loneliness' is mentioned.
It is said of one heroine: 'She is unblemishedly alone'. The figures reject women's roles. They claim that sexuality extinguishes the self, makes
it interchangeable. 'Nothing is more helpless than a being who makes
an issue of its sexuality, it gives way, confuses itself ... ' Helen Meier's
proud position reminds us strikingly of the description of a woman in
a novel of 1928, Meinrad Inglin's *Grand Hotel Excelsior*:

> She had discovered that the important thing for her could not be the relation-
> ship to her parents' house nor to a husband nor to a child, but was solely an
> essential matter which stood beyond all relationships, namely her own self ... The
> feeling arose clearly within her that this world which was dying around her, had
> been a world created by men ...

Helen Meier has a distant relative, as far as the relentlessness and stri-
dency of tone is concerned, in Mariella Mehr. This writer is a 'Jenisch',

as the gypsies call themselves in Switzerland, and understands her origins exclusively from her mother, from whom she was forcibly separated early on and put into a home for 'Children from the Highways'. Accusations against this injustice are to be found explicitly or in concealed form in all her books, from the torero novel *Das Licht der Frau* of 1984 to *Daskind* of 1995.

Born in the 1960s

The radicality of Mariella Mehr, the sovereignty of Helen Meier, and the critical *esprit* and irony of Isolde Schaad, prepared the way for the independence of younger women writers who were first heard in the 1990s. Their role as women is less marked by pain and suffering, but is also less a matter for introspection than was the case with their mothers; the role has a certain self-evident naturalness about it. They were born in the 1960s or at the beginning of the 1970s: Milena Moser, Andrea Simmen, Nicole Müller, Ruth Schweikert, Sabine Reber. The feminine position is for them not the dominant theme, since a place for women has in the meantime been established, even if it is still not a comfortable place. What is noticeable about Milena Moser (born in 1962 in Zürich) is her courage in going for the grotesque, her wit, her pleasure in the absurd, even in the trivial. Andrea Simmen trusts to an unsqueamish, markedly careless prose, which is interlaced with much Zürich-tinged Swiss dialect. Her texts create the effect of having been quickly executed like hard-hitting cartoons. But since the pleasure of destroying is often directed less at the main figures than at what is ruining them, there is much humanity hidden in these wicked sketches. Nicole Müller from Basel (born 1962) first appeared three years ago with a lesbian love-story, *Denn das ist das Schreckliche an der Liebe*, a montage of short prose passages. Müller, however, does not appear to be as carefree as Moser or Simmen: she writes more than they do from a feeling of belonging to a minority.

Ruth Schweikert, twenty-nine at the time, created a sensation at the Literary Festival in Solothurn in 1994 with her story *Christmas* from the collection *Erdnüsse Totschlagen*. Her form of writing was held to be very much of the times; the stories deal with themes currently in discussion, such as Aids, homosexuality, the no–future feeling, drugs, dropouts and – conspicuously – with the rejection of a career, for which, for example, the successful mother of the story, doctor and housewife, had herself striven. This mother has, under constant pressure of time, developed everything except her inner self. She knows neither openness nor motherliness. The contrasts between men and women which were recently still recognisable in literature by women have been replaced in Ruth Schweikert by other areas of pain and tension, even by the drawing of other boundaries. The author follows lines of demarcation which divide society up into a two-thirds society, which splits it into a functioning, working, earning section of the population, and into that other section which falls through the social net, that section with the sick and the addicted. With their often painful truth and their often unsightly poverty, these weaker people, these affected people, point to the inner, spiritual pain of those who conform.

Each of the women writers who has made herself heard in the past quarter of a century certainly stands for herself. The more stringently and the more with an awareness of art these voices are equipped, the more stimulating it is to hear them. Nationality plays a secondary role for the writers themselves; but for readers there is certainly an added attraction in listening, not only to contemporaries, but to women from the same country, to have the atmosphere, the structure of one's own surroundings interpreted or narrated by them. That is perhaps more important than the critical look at Switzerland as a country or as a state which we have been accustomed to for decades from their male Swiss colleagues.

The introduction of female suffrage was, as I have said, not the start of women's literature in Switzerland. Aside from the fact that there had been notable women writers in the first half of the century – above all Regina Ullmann and Cécile Ines Loos – later women writers felt more carried by the age than by political circumstances. So it is no surprise that in the literature by Swiss women writers of the last twenty-five years similar movements of the times manifest themselves as in other countries: in the 1970s a setting forth, often a painful setting forth, into unknown territory; in the 1980s – frequently with second and third books – consolidation, retention or variations on positions already created, tones of one's own; in the 1990s, new, more impertinent sounds and an open questioning of platforms attained, especially as regards assessing issues to do with women.

(Translated by Malcolm Pender)

Bibliography

Theoretical works

Hélène Cixous, *Weiblichkeit in der Schrift*, translated from the French by Eva Duffner (Berlin: 1980)

Hélène Cixous, *Die unendliche Zirkulation des Begehrens* (Berlin: 1977)

Hiltrud Gnüg and Renate Möhrmann (eds.), *Frauenliteraturgeschichte. Schreibende Frauen vom Mittelalter bis zur Gegenwart* (Stuttgart: 1985)

Eidgenössische Kommission für Frauenfragen (ed.), *Die Stellung der Frau in der Schweiz. Bericht der Eidg. Kommission für Frauenfragen,* Part I: *Gesellschaft und Wirtschaft* (1979), Part II: *Biographien und Rollennorm* (1982), Part III: *Recht* (1980), Part IV: *Frauenpolitik* (ca. 1983)

Luce Irigaray, *Speculum. Spiegel des anderen Geschlechts* (Frankfurt/Main: 1980)

Luce Irigaray, *Zur Geschlechterdifferenz. Interviews und Vorträge* (Vienna: 1987)

Julia Kristeva, *Die Revolution der poetischen Sprache* (Frankfurt/Main: 1978)

Klaus Pezold (ed.), *Geschichte der deutschsprachigen Schweizer Literatur im 20. Jahrhundert* (Berlin: 1991)

Gertrud Postl, *Weibliches Sprechen. Feministische Entwürfe zu Sprache und Geschlecht* (Vienna: 1991)

Elsbeth Pulver and Sybille Dallach (eds), *Zwischenzeilen. Schriftstellerinnen der deutschen Schweiz*, Reihe Dossier. Literatur 4 (Pro Helvetia: Zürich/Bern, 1985)

Elisabeth Ryter *et al.* (eds), *Und schrieb und schrieb sie wie ein Tiger aus dem Busch. Über Schriftstellerinnen in der deutschsprachigen Schweiz* (Zürich: 1994)

Sigrid Weigel, *Die Stimme der Medusa. Schreibweisen in der Gegenwartsliteratur von Frauen* (Reinbek: 1989)

Susanna Woodtli, *Gleichberechtigung. Der Kampf um die politischen Rechte der Frau in der Schweiz* (Frauenfeld: 1983)

Literary works

Margrit Baur, *Von Strassen, Plätzen und ferneren Umständen* (Frankfurt/Main: 1971)
Margrit Baur, *Überleben. Eine unsystematische Ermittlung gegen die Not aller Tage,*
	(Frankfurt/Main: 1981)
Margrit Baur, *Geschichtenflucht* (Frankfurt/Main: 1988)
Margrit Baur, *Alle Herrlichkeit* (Frankfurt/Main: 1993)
Maja Beutler, *Flissingen fehlt auf der Karte* (Bern: 1976)
Maja Beutler, *Fuss fassen* (Bern: 1980)
Maja Beutler, *Die Wortfalle* (Bern: 1983)
Maja Beutler, *Das Bildnis der Doña Quichotte* (Zürich: 1989)
Alice Ceresa, *La figlia prodiga* (Turin: 1967)
Anne Cuneo, *Mortelle Maladie* (1969), translated from the French by Pierre Imhasly
	as *Dinge, bedeckt mit Schatten* (Zürich: 1975)
Adelheid Duvanel, *Windgeschichten* (Darmstadt: 1980)
Adelheid Duvanel, *Anna und ich* (Darmstadt: 1985)
Adelheid Duvanel, *Das verschwundene Haus* (Darmstadt: 1988)
Adelheid Duvanel, *Die Brieffreundin* (München: 1995)
Anna Felder, *Umzug durch die Katzentür,* translated from the Italian by Maria Spre-
	cher (Zürich: 1975)
Eveline Hasler, *Anna Göldin. Letzte Hexe* (Zürich: 1982)
Eveline Hasler, *Die Wachsflügelfrau. Geschichte der Emily Kempin-Spyri* (Zürich: 1991)
Rahel Hutmacher, *Doña* (Darmstadt: 1982)
Rahel Hutmacher, *Tochter* (Darmstadt: 1983)
Meinrad Inglin, *Grand Hotel Excelsior* (Zürich: 1928)
Hanna Johansen, *Die stehende Uhr* (Munich: 1978)
Hanna Johansen, *Die Analphabetin* (Munich: 1982)
Hanna Johansen, *Über den Wunsch sich wohlzufühlen* (Munich: 1985)
Monique Laederach, *L'Etain et la Source* (Lausanne: 1970)
Gertrud Leutenegger, *Vorabend* (Frankfurt/Main: 1975)
Gertrud Leutenegger, *Gouverneur* (Frankfurt/Main: 1981)
Gertrud Leutenegger, *Meduse* (Frankfurt/Main: 1988)
Gertrud Leutenegger, *Acheron* (Frankfurt/Main: 1994)
Mariella Mehr, *Steinzeit* (Zürich: 1980)
Mariella Mehr, *Das Licht der Frau. Spanien und spanische Stierkämpferinnen* (Zürich:
	1984)
Mariella Mehr, *Daskind* (Zürich: 1995)
Helen Meier, *Trockenwiese* (Zürich: 1984)
Helen Meier, *Das Haus am See* (Zürich: 1987)
Helen Meier, *Lebenleben* (Zürich: 1989)
Milena Moser, *Gebrochene Herzen* (Zürich: 1990)
Milena Moser, *Das Schlampenbuch* (Zürich: 1992)
Milena Moser, *Blondinenträume* (Hamburg: 1994)
Nicole Müller, *Denn das ist das Schreckliche an der Liebe* (Zürich: 1992)

Erica Pedretti, *Harmloses, bitte* (Frankfurt/Main: 1970)
Erica Pedretti, *Valerie oder das unerzogene Auge* (Frankfurt/Main: 1986)
Isolde Schaad, *Knowhow am Klimasndschane* (Zürich: 1980)
Isolde Schaad, *Küsschen Tschüss* (Zürich: 1989)
Isolde Schaad, *Body & Sofa. Liebesgeschichten aus der Kaufkraftklasse* (Zürich: 1994)
Margrit Schriber, *Vogel flieg* (Frauenfeld: 1980)
Margrit Schriber, *Muschelgarten* (Zürich: 1984)
Ruth Schweikert, *Erdnüsse. Totschlagen* (Zürich: 1994)
Andrea Simmen, *Ich bin ein Opfer des Doppelpunkts* (Frankfurt/Main: 1991)
Verena Stefan, *Häutungen* (Berlin: 1982)
Laure Wyss, *Weggehen ehe das Meer gefriert* (Zürich: 1994)

Agnès Cardinal

Reclaiming the Past: Recent Writings by German-speaking Swiss Women

When, in 1972, the novelist Irmtraud Morgner was asked about her underlying motivation, her reply was categorical and immediate. What prompted her to write, she said, was the need to bring about the 'Eintritt der Frau in die Historie'.[1] In the forum of public discourse, she argued, the majority of women have so far remained silent. In consequence they have played virtually no active role in the shaping of the histories, the myths, the debates, indeed, the general culture of mankind. Writing, Morgner insists, must be understood as a political act. By its very nature, a text demands to be read. It is created in order to gain access to the public domain where it will contribute to a shared body of opinions, attitudes and knowledge. To write, therefore, is to make use of a kind of 'Stimmrecht' of the creative mind.

For twenty-five years now, Swiss women have had the vote: that is, they have had the right to respond with a bare 'yes' or 'no' to strategically formulated questions. Essential though this may have been for the enhancement, in recent years, of the status and influence of women in Swiss communal life, the political vote represents only one facet of true emancipation. What needs to be recognised as of equal, if not superior, importance, is the impact on the body politic which women make when they begin to write, when they publish their works and, above all, when they succeed in interesting a sizeable readership in their stories, their histories and myths, their fantasies and fictions. It is therefore extremely encouraging to note that, over the last thirty years or so, more and more books by German-Swiss women have appeared on the shelves of bookshops and libraries, not just in Switzerland but in the German-speaking world at large, and even further afield. The sheer variety of these writings is proof that Swiss women have much to say and

---

1 Joachim Walther, 'Interview mit Irmtraud Morgner' in *Weltbühne*, no.32 (1972), p. 1011.

that, at last, they are beginning to say it publicly. More often than not, however, their texts tend to be treated as curiosities and housed on shelves designated for 'Swiss Authors' or worse still, 'Swiss Women Authors'. What remains to be achieved, surely, is the unmitigated integration of such writing within the general body of literary production. Only when the ghettoisation of a book on the basis of the gender or ethnic origin of its author is no longer practised can a text, any text, assume its rightful place in the forum of cultural discourse.

Two reasons prompted me to begin my reflections on recent German-Swiss women's writing with a quotation from beyond the Swiss border. The first is my wish to pay tribute to the East German writer Irmtraud Morgner, who like no-one else has given thought, voice and narrative shape to the general politics of women's writing. Her notion of the 'Eintritt der Frau in die Historie' will be a central concern in my deliberations here.

The second reason corresponds, as I have already indicated, to my inclination to resist the notion that the writing of German-Swiss women should somehow be set apart from any other writing. It is true, of course, that in political and historical terms, Switzerland is a unique case. The critic Ann Marie Rasmussen states what no-one will dispute when she writes that 'shielded from the devastations of the First and Second World Wars, and only intermittently touched by their moral and political consequences, [Switzerland] has emerged as a society where continuity rather than disruption is the norm, and where traditional values, particularly regarding the status of women, are strong.'[2] But while it is relatively easy to identify the historical and political factors which shape a country's culture, it is infinitely more difficult to connect that culture in any significant way to the tropes of artistic production. Invariably the attempt to draw easy parallels between Switzerland's political reality and the nature and development of its literature remains questionable.[3] To be sure, many Swiss writers – from Johann Bodmer

2 Ann Marie Rasmussen, 'Women and Literature in German-Speaking Switzerland: Tendencies in the 1980s' in *Amsterdamer Beiträge zur neueren Germanistik*, vol. 29, 1989, pp. 159–160.

3 For a recent attempt to do this see Hans-Peter Ecker 'Blick über den Rhein' in *Literatur aus der Schweiz: Passauer Pegasus. Zeitschrift für Literatur*, 11, 21/22 (1993), pp. 25–45. In this otherwise extremely persuasive article on writings by

and Johanna Spyri to Max Frisch have, at some stage in their lives, written about Switzerland or the experience of Swissness. There is nothing intrinsically odd about this. Such writers draw upon personal experience in the same way that Günter Grass does for his fictions about his native Danzig, or Elfriede Jelinek in her treatment of contemporary Austria. What must be challenged, though, is the critic's determination to track down, in the variety of artistic expressions originating from a given fund of collective socio-political experience, a 'family similarity' or 'sibling sensibility' which is alleged to manifest itself in a shared theme or typifying form. Thus when, in evaluating some recent fictions by German-Swiss women, Rasmussen draws a connection between the conservative nature of Swiss society and the 'disquieting presence' of convention and an affirmation of the traditional role of women,[4] one might well want to point out that women's novels which confirm a conventional view of the role of women are hardly unique to German-speaking Switzerland. Gabriele Wohmann, Elisabeth Plessen and Ursula Krechel, all of whom live and work in Germany, have for decades written fictions which move within very similar parameters to those of Maja Beutler, Gertrud Leutenegger and Margrit Schriber. Furthermore – and even within the narrow confines of the literature by Swiss Germanophone women – the range of themes, attitudes and ideas is so vast and varied that any generalizing theory can always be undone through examples which prove the opposite. For example, it is an often reiterated claim that since 1971 the fictions of the post-war generation of German-Swiss women have been marked by an obsession with 'a Drang zur Selbst-Verwirklichung' and a certain feministoid 'Wehleidigkeit'. Granted, there do exist such novels, but there also others which deal with radically different concerns. Erika Pedretti, for one, has published

---

Geiser, Kirchhoff and Burger, Ecker 'möchte [...] die These aufstellen, daß der häufig konstatierend von Lesern zumeist intuitiv wahrgenommene "Realismus-gehalt" großer Teile der Schweizer Gegenwartsliteratur [...] *auch* darauf beruht, daß die Schweizer Autoren [...] nicht in dem Maße in einen durchrationalisier-ten Medienbetrieb intregriert sind wie ihre deutschen oder gar amerikanischen Kollegen.' (p. 31) The connection between "Realismusgehalt" of a novel and the "Medienbetrieb" might not strike everyone as straightforward as Ecker believes it to be.

4 Rasmussen, p. 182.

several works which clearly rank among the most intriguing contributions to contemporary avant-garde writing. Her *Sebastian* (1973), for
example, or *Die Veränderung oder die Zertrümmerung von dem Kind Karl
und anderen Personen* (1977), and the even more extraordinary *Valerie oder
Das unerzogene Auge* (1986), are literary explorations of consciousness
and ways of seeing which reach far beyond gender-specific concerns.
In a similar vein, it would be quite inappropriate to link the delicately
honed expressions of the poet Erika Burkart concerning, for example,
her intensely personal relationship with the landscape of her native
Aargau, to any political or cultural agenda.

Two misleading truisms about the nature of contemporary Germanophone Swiss women's fiction are currently in circulation. The first sug-
gests that by virtue of their very origin, such texts must be of limited
interest and appeal only to the 'connoisseur'. The second claims that
today's German-speaking Swiss women have no idea how to tell a good
story. Both can be refuted by citing the example of Eveline Hasler. Two
of her novels, *Anna Göldin. Letzte Hexe*[5] (1982) and *Die Wachsflügelfrau*[6]
(1991) have become bestsellers at home and abroad precisely because
they tell a gripping yarn. These books are of such general as well as academic interest that they have quickly established themselves as set books
on the syllabuses of schools and colleges. Hasler's novels are significant
not least because they reach a wide and varied readership.

It is not difficult to account for the success of *Anna Göldin. Letzte
Hexe*. Hasler's reconstruction of the career of Anna Göldin, the last
woman to be executed as a witch in Switzerland, is indeed spellbind-
ing. Of course, stories about witches, and generally about women who
transgress, have always been popular. In our feminist age the figure of
the witch in particular has achieved special status as an icon of dissent
and a symbol of subversive feminine power. Quite apart from telling a
fascinating story, Hasler's novel thus responds, in more ways than one,
to a mood and an interest of our time, even if it soon becomes obvious that the reconstruction of the fate of the witch Anna Göldin is
unlikely to confirm any romantic notion a reader might want to nur-
ture about the power of witches.

5 Eveline Hasler, *Anna Göldin. Letzte Hexe* (Zürich/Köln: Benziger, 1982).
6 Eveline Hasler, *Die Wachsflügelfrau* (Zürich/Frauenfeld: Nagel & Kimche, 1991).

The real-life story of Anna Göldin can be told in a few sentences. She was born in 1734 into a peasant family eking out a living on the stony slopes of the Glarus mountains. Diligent and agile of mind, she began to earn her own living while still a child, first as a farm hand, and later as a domestic servant. Eventually she was promoted to the position of maid and indispensable *factotum* in the house of the physician and town elder Melchior Tschudi in the town of Glarus. At the age of forty-eight, on 18 June 1782, she met her death by the sword in the town square. She had been tried and found guilty of having corrupted the nine-year old daughter of her employer by means of putting pieces of metal into her food, so that, for weeks and in great pain, the child vomited pins and needles, large nails and sections of wire.

A psychologist and a historian by training, Eveline Hasler anchors her narrative in documentary evidence, gleaned from church registers, archives and transcripts of the trial proceedings, and relates the bizarre facts of Anna's crime, torture, trial and execution with an eerie impassivity. In a kind of *erlebte Rede*, the narrative voice sometimes seems to belong to Anna, sometimes to another protagonist; more often it is that of an objective latterday narrator. On occasion it assumes collective status when the entire population of Glarus seems to converge to vocalise those unfocused, semi-conscious thought-processes which ultimately will bring about the gruesome and cruel death of one of their own. These many voices, interspersed with direct quotations from archival material and vivid period detail, combine to create a literary tableau brimming with the atmosphere of that distant place and time.

The novel assumes further dimensions as Hasler surreptitiously links the strange goings-on in the dark rooms of the Tschudi household to a wider historical and political context. The witch Anna Göldin was born into the century of the Enlightenment. It was a time when the prosperous burghers of Zürich, who themselves had fought hard for their own freedom, had become the bailiffs of Glarus. With the help of their vassals as well as local dignitaries, these burghers assiduously collect their dues from the impoverished peasants, whose desperate survival strategies Hasler evokes in a series of harrowing sketches sharpened by her terse style. The cumulative effect of these cameos of oppression is to make visible the ways in which man-made poverty leads to suppressed anger, harshness of manners, fear, superstition and violence. Without commentary and in an apparently non-judgemental way, Hasler also shows how, in far-away Zürich, no-one feels responsible for the murderous drama developing in Glarus. When news of Anna's trial reaches the wider world, the fair-minded townspeople of Zürich are anxious to limit their involvement to an expression of outrage at the unenlightened barbarism rampant in the mountains.

Anna Göldin. Letzte Hexe is not only a fascinating reconstruction of events which ultimately led to the execution of one unfortunate woman, it is also a convincing study of the workings of power, and of male power at that. Hasler's eighteenth-century Glarus is a sombre place. It is a world where poverty, fear and repressed sexual energies meet up with the powers of a ruthless masculine imperialism to create an atmosphere in which the voices of reason and tolerance fall silent, children spit nails and women turn into witches. As such the book is not just a historical tableau or a political thriller, it also makes a comment, still valid in our age, on the dire consequences of heedless sexual and economic exploitation.

Following the success of *Anna Göldin*, Eveline Hasler embarked on the reclamation from the past of another Swiss woman's life. *Die Wachsflügelfrau* is the story of Emily Kempin-Spyri, the world's first woman lawyer. Unlike Anna Göldin, who was well established in the Helvetic imagination as one of the more colourful figures in its history, Dr Emily Kempin-Spyri was, until recently, virtually unknown. Hasler's research brings to light documents which state that Emilie Spyri was born in Zürich in 1853, the daughter of Johann Ludwig Spyri, assistant vicar of the parish of Altstetten near Zürich. In 1883 she married the clergyman Walter Kempin, had three children and, five years later, became the first woman to obtain a doctorate in Jurisprudence from Zürich University. She subsequently emigrated to the United States, taking her husband and three children with her. In 1885, under the auspices of the University of New York, she founded a successful law school for women. She published a large body of texts on legal matters, and, upon her return to Europe, became a *Privatdozentin* at the Universities of Zürich, Berlin and Dresden.

In view of such achievements one might well expect this account of a woman's career to evoke a saner, sunnier world than that of an eighteenth-century witch in Glarus. The 'Wings of Wax' of the title and the recurring reference to Icarus throughout the narrative should warn the reader against any such sanguine assumptions. Hasler begins her account of Emily Kempin's career in the year 1899, two years before her death. We meet her in a cell in the psychiatric clinic of Friedmatt in Basel, where, riddled with cancer, penniless, and recently certified insane after a nervous breakdown, she spends her time cutting figures out of magazines and devising futile schemes of escape. Echoing her technique in *Anna Göldin. Letzte Hexe*, Hasler adopts a method of literary *montage* in which pure fiction, imagined scenes and conversations, as well as the narrator's musings about the woman's life, are anchored in quotations from all manner of contemporary sources, notably newspapers and other archival documents unearthed in libraries in Zürich, Berlin and New York. These are complemented by quotations from lucky discoveries such as an odd letter by Ricarda Huch and – most poignant of all – six undelivered letters which Kempin penned in Friedmatt shortly before she died. Anecdotes, roughly sketched, are put into relief by the terse asides of the modern narrator whose light-beam focus skips backwards and forwards along the chronology of her heroine's life. What emerges is an intermittent outline of Emily Kempin's story in the general context of late nineteenth-century culture. Yet the narrative constantly alerts the reader to the modern-day bias which has influenced and shaped this sample of reclaimed past. It is perhaps inevitable, therefore, that Hasler's evocation of Zürich and New York in the 1880s should remain rather shadowy and somewhat sparsely furnished in terms of period detail. Indeed, the narrative relies a little too much on the suggestive power of a handful of famous people, for many of New York's most intriguing late nineteenth century glitterati appear as names gratuitously dropped into Emily Kempin's orbit. Similarly the intrigues amongst council members during the heroine's early married life in the parish of Zürich-Enge are very sketchily drawn and provide the vaguest political backdrop to the heroine's struggle. Hasler comes into her own, however, when her imagination begins to draw together metaphor and reality to lend the story a subliminal poetic dimension. For instance, Enge – originally just the name of an affluent parish – becomes the watchword for the entire story of Kempin's life. In New York, the word acquires extended meaning through a glimpse of a group of nameless immigrants who, on stifling-hot summer nights, take to sleeping on fire escapes and flat roofs. Wrapped in their mosquito nets, they lie about in the darkened cityscape like luminous pupae. As such they are almost tangible evocations of that atmosphere, ever present in the narrative, of suffocating oppression and the terror of not being quite ready for the challenge. It is a state of being whereby 'gegen die Enge atmen'[7] remains the sole means of survival.

Even so, much of the interest of the book resides in the way the heroine's struggle is situated within the force-field of the conflicting social and economic energies which characterize Swiss society in the mid-nineteenth century. For example, Johann Spyri, Emily's autocratic father, begins his career as a clergyman and ends up working as a stat-istician, helping with the planning and supervision of the new railway which enters the Zürich landscape. He stands in a revealing contra-puntal relationship to the other clergyman in Emily's life, her Prussian husband Walter Kempin, a mild-mannered idealist whose progressive philanthropic projects have a way of turning to dust and who, to the dismay of old Spyri, allows his wife to enrol as a student at the local university. Yet the most interesting aspect of Hasler's tableau of life in the nineteenth century is the way she situates Emily Kempin's career alongside that other contemporary women of note. Emily's aunt, the author Johanna Spyri, appears in a cameo role as an aloof and deeply conservative figure, sternly unsympathetic to her niece's ambitions. There is a reference too, to Lydia Escher, the tragic daughter of the great industrialist Alfred Escher, who, when caught in Rome while trying to elope with a painter, was declared insane and spent the rest of her life under house arrest in the family villa on Lake Zürich. Hasler also makes mention of Caroline Farner, one of the first female doc-tors in Switzerland, who was arrested and imprisoned in Zürich on trumped-up charges which were later publicly and embarrassingly challenged by the redoubtable feminist and aristocrat Meta von Salis. Indeed, it is one of the delights of the book that it makes visible, al-beit only in fleeting allusions, the paradoxes that shaped life in a town like Zürich in the 1880s. Provincial, conservative and cautious on the one hand, Zürich was also a place sizzling with the ferment of progress. The liberal policies of its university – one of the first in Europe to

7   Eveline Hasler, *Die Wachsflügelfrau*, p. 144.

admit women students – were well in advance of their time. Thus Zürich became the unlikely venue for the congregation of Europe's most progressive women. In a number of gently amusing asides, Hasler evokes the discomfiture of its citizens at the sight of bevies of red-stockinged Russian women flocking up the Zürcherberg on their way to their classes. Amid the students attending Dr Emily Kempin's lecture on *Women and the Law*, we glimpse the earnest countenance of a young Polish exilee named Rosa Luxemburg and learn that, when Emily Kempin celebrates a first academic success, Ricarda Huch (who had obtained her history doctorate only a year before) sends a feminist poem but declines the invitation because she abhors public festivities in any form.

Trivial though they may seem, such anecdotes resonate in the mind of today's female reader. It is precisely in mundane detail that she can begin to recognize the reality of women's historical past. In the preamble to *Die Wachsflügelfrau*, Hasler relates that when she started researching Kempin's biography, she encountered obstacles everywhere. No record, for example, not even a 'Personalkarte', could be unearthed to authenticate her heroine's confinement in the Friedmatt clinic. Frau Kempin, geborene Spyri, Doctor jur., was, it seemed to her, 'eine Frau die von ihrer Zeit nicht vorgesehen war, und die es heute, hundert Jahre später, immer noch nicht geben darf.' 'Es gibt sie doch'[8] is the defiant reaction from which Hasler's project draws its narrative impetus.

This determination to excavate the stories of our female antecedents from beneath the cultural debris of prejudice and indifference seems to engage the best and most compelling narrative impulses in women writers of our age. Naturally, this is as true of Swiss women as it is of women writers world-wide.[9] It is a process in which the dry and diligent assemblage of historical data seems invariably to release a flamboyant

---

8 Eveline Hasler, *Die Wachsflügelfrau*, p. 6.
9 Among the most famous examples are Christa Wolf, *Kein Ort. Nirgends* (1979), or *Kassandra* (1983), Irmtraud Morgner, *Leben und Abenteuer der Trobadora Beatriz* (1974), or Brigitte Struzyk, *Caroline unterm Freiheitsbaum* (1988). It is perhaps indicative that some of the most interesting texts of this kind originated in the GDR where women understood themselves as participants in the construction of a new society.

surge of the imagination, endowing the spectres of times long past with a palpably modern aura of myth, fancy and glamour.

That imagination, and a 'Lust zum Fabulieren', are essential to the project of reclaiming women's lost ancestry. When Elisabeth Joris and Heidi Witzi published their highly successful survey of two centuries of Swiss women's history, they chose for its title the telling formula *Frauengeschichte – Frauengeschichten*.[10] Their book is but one example of the rich harvest of the last twenty-five years, in which publications of every kind, documentary, historical, fictional, and mixtures of all three, have set out to relate the history of women. In their entirety they have brought before the public gaze a veritable 'Ahnengalerie' of remarkable women from Switzerland's past. When I went to school in Zürich in the 1950s, none of us Daughters of Zürich had the slightest inkling of the existence of local heroines like Anna Waser, the enigmatic seventeenth-century painter, or of Regula Engel, who fought side by side with her husband on the Napoleonic battlefields, gave birth to twenty-one children and, after her husband's death, kept herself out of the poorhouse by publishing the memoirs of a 'schweizerische Amazone'.[11]

There are now new and enterprising publishers such as the 'efef Verlag' in Zürich who are re-issuing all but forgotten books by all but forgotten Swiss women authors. Their edition of Lina Bögli's *Talofa*,[12] for instance, makes once more available what, early this century, was an international best-seller. First issued in English in 1905 under the title *Forward!*, it relates Bögli's ten years of solitary globetrotting in Australia and New Zealand, and across the South Seas to North America. Many other texts of this kind await discovery. There are the writings of the waitress Annelise Rüegg, who spent the First World War giving impromptu lectures on the merits of socialism and pacifism in the parks and on the street corners of Paris, London and New York, was arrested in Germany for smuggling food to Russian prisoners of war, and was finally deported to Switzerland from the United States

10 *Frauengeschichte(n): Dokumente aus zwei Jahrhunderten zur Situation der Frauen in der Schweiz*, (Zürich: Limmat Verlag, 1986).
11 Cf. Regula Engel-Egli, *Frau Oberst Engel. Memoiren einer Amazone aus Napoleonischer Zeit*, (Zürich: Limmat Verlag, 1992).
12 Lina Bögli, *Talofa*, (Zürich: efef Verlag, 1990).

for preaching peace outside a church in Massachusetts.[13] Research is only just beginning on the intriguing figure of Olga Plümacher-Hünerwadel, native of Lenzburg, aunt of Franz Wedekind, and author of a series of complex philosophical tracts composed in the mid-nineteenth century in a remote Tennessee farmhouse.

The reclamation from the past of figures such as these is, there can be no doubt, an essential aspect of the coming of age of women of today. If they are to take their rightful place in the public domain, women need to be able draw courage and inspiration from mother figures and role models from their past. Indeed the historical dimension is a crucial aspect of the consolidation of a present identity. This holds true for the public sphere as it does for the private and is particularly important in our fluid modern world where alienation reigns and where the sense of rootedness has become a scarce commodity. Like so many others in this modern world, the Swiss woman will be seeking in the portraits of her ancestors that *Doppelgänger* from another age in whose features she can recognize the traits of her own identity, and whose story will help her to grasp the topography of her present culture.

It is in the context of that search for a role model or mother figure that I would finally like to draw attention to a recent work by Verena Stefan. Stefan, one may recall, won international notoriety in the 1970s with *Häutungen*,[14] an uncompromising experimental text celebrating feminism and lesbianism. It is both poignant and significant that, twenty years after that initial rebellion, and having encountered considerable difficulties in her attempts at forging, single-handedly, a Germanic 'écriture féminine',[15] Stefan should now have come to write a simple and meditative book about her mother. The slender volume is called *Es ist reich gewesen*,[16] a phrase apparently uttered by her mother when talking about her life shortly before she died. Stefan's book is a 'kaddish', a lament on a death. It is equally a tracing of the troubled lineage from a daughter to her mother and on back to a grandmother almost lost in time.

---

13 Cf. Annelise Rüegg, *Im Kriege durch die Welt*, (Zürich: Grütli-Buchhandlung, 1918).

14 Verena Stefan, *Häutungen* (Berlin: Frauenoffensive, 1975).

15 Cf Verena Stefan, *Wortgetreu ich träume: Geschichten und Geschichte* (Zürich: Arche Verlag, 1987).

16 Verena Stefan, *Es ist reich gewesen* (Frankfurt/Main: Fischer, 1993).

We are told how Verena Stefan's mother hid a set of secret diaries deep in her linen chest. In these she had chronicled, once husband and children were away, the comings and goings of forty years of family life, compiling records of her cooking and cleaning, and on occasion giving vent to fury or despair at a life entirely spent as the keeper of the house. The book is both a tribute to this hidden œuvre and a comment on the problematic relationship which women have traditionally had to the written word. Stefan dedicates her text to her Bernese grandmother – who was forbidden, even, to *read* novels, and to her mother, who wrote in secret in order to survive. The very existence of Verena Stefan's book is an index of the spectacular progress Swiss women have made, in only three generations, on the long road to full political and spiritual emancipation.

Erika Swales

'Wörter, die man schluckt, werden lebendig':
Reflections on Eveline Hasler's *Anna Göldin Letzte Hexe*

Eveline Hasler's novels written between 1979 and 1988 stand out by their increasing preoccupation with the theme of emancipation, the individual and collective quest for liberation. The sheer pace of her critically engaged development is impressive: *Novemberinsel*, 1979, is an 'Erzählung', rooted in the purely subjective and is set within familiar, but narrow feminist territory – the married woman in search of personal identity, freedom. Hildegard, mother of four children, worn out by the sheer monotony of daily life, makes a last dash for 'meine einzige Überlebenschance' (p. 39) by retreating with her youngest child to an Italian island. The attempt is doomed as the very semantics of the title suggest: unable to cut the umbilical cord of motherhood, Hildegard returns at the end to an uncertain future. Overall, the work hardly moves beyond these parameters: whilst Erica Pedretti's novel *Die Zertrümmerung von dem Kind Karl* (1977), subtitled 'Veränderung', fully turns on the issue of change, *Novemberinsel* figures as but another variation on the familiar theme of 'Ferien vom Ich'.

It is with the move from *story* to *history* that Hasler's particular energy comes into its own. The focus point of *Anna Göldin Letzte Hexe* (1982), *Ibicaba – Das Paradies in den Köpfen* (1985), and *Der Riese im Baum* (1988), decisively shifts from the subjective to the objective, historical world. All three novels acknowledge the force of history in that they are underpinned by extensive research; at the same time Hasler asserts her own voice by critically reworking and elaborating on the exclusively male perspectives of her source material. Her archaeological re-tracing consistently combines with a sharply probing critique of precise political, economic and cultural conditions which generate, yet ultimately militate against, the quest for emancipation. With this specific thematic engagement, Hasler situates herself in a long literary tradition. In the second half of the twentieth century, the issue of personal

and social transformation has been at the forefront of women's writing
– one thinks, for example, of Anna Seghers, Ingeborg Bachmann, Christa
Wolf and, most recently, Elfriede Jelinek. It is against this background
that, in the following, I want to focus on the novel *Anna Göldin Letzte
Hexe*. I hope to show that Hasler's *mode* of writing combines a fierce
socio-political analysis with a feminist dimension.

The novel turns on a decisive moment in European cultural history
– the trial, torture and execution of a witch in 1782, the heyday of the
Enlightenment. Anna Göldin, having grown up in utter poverty, makes
her living as a maid. Her last post is in the house of the wealthy, respected doctor Tschudi in Glarus. Her reticently proud demeanour and
beauty create an atmosphere of tension from the start, and she is finally
accused of witchcraft when one of her charges – nine year old Anna
Maria – begins to spit pins and nails and increasingly suffers from con-
vulsions. Backed up by substantial source material, the novel employs
the particular case to illuminate the political and cultural tensions of the
years leading up to the French Revolution. The valley of Glarus figures as a perfect paradigm for the 'unsicheren Zeitläuften' (p. 104), the
conflict between political and cultural tradition on the one hand and
the claims of enlightenment, emancipation, on the other. The dark
forces win, but, as Hasler reminds us, the trial and execution of Anna
Göldin made history in contemporary Germany: writers and scholars
denounced the abuse of justice and coined the term 'Justizmord' (p. 221).
By contrast, Swiss voices kept quiet, and in Glarus the original documents disappeared immediately after the trial. In this sense, Hasler's novel
makes up for a blatant gap in Swiss consciousness: 'Auf Annas Spuren'
(p. 7), it speaks up where there was silence. But the novel moves well
beyond the reconstruction of a judicial scandal: the specific is height-
ened into an indictment of a repressive political and cultural system. To
this degree, Hasler's account recalls Maria Waser's novel *Die Geschichte
der Anna Waser* (1959), set in 17th century Switzerland. Here, too, the
execution of a 'Hexe' serves to generate vehement protest and opens the
protagonist's eyes to the necessity of enlightenment – 'ja, ihre Augen
wollten andere Zeiten sehen' (p. 102).

Anna Göldin Letzte Hexe systematically lays bare the power structures
which pervade the economy of both private and public politics. Here,
Hasler is not alone – in many ways her work connects with those strands

of twentieth Swiss women's writing and research which trace the history of maids driven to infanticide by intolerable conditions. But *Anna Göldin Letzte Hexe* goes further: numerous passages, ceaselessly shifting back and forth in Anna's life and held in a tenor of laconic pathos, capture a monstrous social order which rests on the masses of the dispossessed and disempowered. In this context Hasler's handling of punctuation attains a particular significance: she restricts her use of quotation marks to archival and literary material, and thereby she ensures that individual speech is depersonalized. As in *Der Riese im Baum*, dialogue becomes transparent upon the attitudinal discourse of the times. At the same time the absence of quotation marks facilitates the modulation into free indirect speech, allowing the narrative voice to partake fully of the protagonist's sense of anger and outrage. This is further reflected in structural terms: the solidity of paragraphs, of stable objective account, is throughout countermanded by the highly charged rhythm of percussion-like one-liners which capture the hectic pulse of horror.

In stylistic terms, the particular force of the novel derives from Hasler's use of leitmotifs. In part this can be traced back to *Novemberinsel* where the motif of water seeping through the walls and roof of Hildegard's temporary safe haven generates an increasing sense of threat. But given the narrow focus of this story, the potential of the leitmotif cannot fully develop. By contrast, in *Anna Göldin Letzte Hexe* Hasler's metaphorical technique is reminiscent of Brecht's 'Gestus' theory in that the leitmotifs encapsulate the prevailing power relations. The argument of the novel turns on the central idea of domination, the 'Netz' of 'Herrschaft' (p. 136). Accordingly, the term 'Herr' covers the entire spectrum of power, ranging from the 'Hausherr' and 'Dienstherr' to the 'Ratsherren', masters of the public political realm, and finally to the 'Chorherren', the patriarchs of the spiritual order – Johann Caspar Lavater, the shadow of Calvin, and, ultimately, God. As in *Die Geschichte der Anna Waser*, the 'heilige Obrigkeit' and 'hohe Geistlichkeit' (p. 101) are seen to preserve the repressive status quo. Whilst the establishment celebrates Lavater as the passionate advocate of humanity – of 'Herz, Gefühl' (p. 48) – he figures for the servants as the author of a 'Sittenbüchlein für das Gesinde'. His instructions preach humble submission in the name of a divinely appointed order: 'Gottes alles leitende Fürsehung wollte, daß du ein Dienstbote seyst' (p. 49) and 'Die Stimme deiner Herrschaft ... soll dir

seyn wie die Stimme Gottes ... ' (p. 53). Clustered around this central
idea of 'Herrschaft' there are the all-pervasive motifs of property and
power on the one hand – 'gehören', 'Recht', 'auf obrigkeitlichen Be-
fehl' (p. 62) – and on the other hand particles of deprivation, disem-
powerment – 'unfrei', 'Abhängigkeit' (p. 7), 'verschuldet' (p. 63), 'die
Stummheit, das Schweigen, sich ducken' (p. 122). Measured against the
inescapable force of these opposing blocks, Anna Göldin's quest for
change is a priori doomed. She is determined to transcend the law of
stones – 'Das Gesetz der Steine aufheben, die dort liegenbleiben, wo
sie hinfallen' (p. 9) – but the narrative is shot through with the motif
of stones as emblems of irreducible given conditions, the insuperable
walls of poverty and social divisions – 'Grenze an Grenze, bis zu den
Flanken des Bergs' (p. 31).

Anna Göldin Letzte Hexe relates the defeat of emancipatory energies.
Anna's yearning for 'die neue Zeit' (p. 104), her 'Drang, sich zu ver-
ändern' (p. 9), is irrevocably doomed and as such prefigures almost lit-
erally the central theme of a desperate 'Drang nach Veränderung' (p. 23)
in Hasler's next novel, *Ibicaba – Das Paradies in den Köpfen*, which is set
in the nineteenth century. The vision of historical change is urgently
present throughout – there are numerous references to Jean-Jacques
Rousseau, in particular his *contrat social* – but, as in *Die Geschichte der Anna
Waser*, the 'neue Zeit' is but a vision, 'wie aus Büchern abgeschrieben'
(p. 190). Thus, inspired by the idealism of Melchior, her former master and lover, Anna dreams of a paradisal future in 1982 (p. 104), of
metamorphosis which would transform historically defined selfhood
into a 'Falter, der um Mitternacht aus dem sich öffnenden Kelch der
Tulpe fliegt, blaue Blitzspur, Irrlicht' (pp. 36–7) – but these dreams figure as the lyricisms of a false paradise, a theme which lies at the very heart
of *Ibicaba – Das Paradies in den Köpfen*. If there is an intimation of change
it is to be found in the recurrent references to violent forces. The motif
of arson, fire, is associated with political unrest threatening the established
order, as in Selina Chönz's *Der Besuch* (1979), or, in much more height-
ened form, in Gertrud Leutenegger's *Das verlorene Monument* (1979). Similarly, the motif of storms, the 'Föhn', clearly links with the prospect of
revolution, the 'Wirbelsturm, der aus Frankreich kommt' (p. 154).

As these examples suggest, the *polemical* voice of the novel uses numerous motifs which highlight the order of a repressive socio-political,

economic and cultural regime. To this degree they are *mono-valent* – this is to say: their metaphorical referentiality is stable. This also applies to the patterns which encapsulate the tensions between tradition and innovation. Felicity Rash has shown in detail how, for example, the elements of light and darkness foreground the persistent currents and counter-currents of superstition and enlightenment. Such mono-valent motifs exert, then, considerable critical force. But I want to suggest that they are only part of the text's import. More complexly, we find trains of *poly-valent* images which redraw the battle-lines of the polemical statement: centring on the issues of sexuality and pregnancy, these images generate a set of differentiated reflections on patterns of repression and expression. Within this perspective, the figures of Frau Tschudi and her daughter Anna Maria on the one hand and Anna Göldin on the other are re-aligned: the configuration of opposition, of mistress versus servant, modulates into one of parallels, even of kinship.

On the overt level, Dr Tschudi and his wife figure, of course, as 'Herr' and 'Herrin' over Anna Göldin, who is part of their property. Antagonism and anxiety are overt within this relationship: Frau Tschudi is immediately haunted by a 'beklemmender Gedanke ... Schon der Gestalt nach nimmt diese Frau doppelt soviel Raum ein wie sie selbst' (p. 13), and there is an ominous note to her friends' comment: 'Heutzutage muß man zweimal hinschauen, um herauszufinden, wer Herrin, wer Dienstbote ist' (p. 14). The Hegelian dialectic of the master/slave relationship is to invade the marital bedroom quite explicitly: 'Noch nie hatte eine Magd ihre Herrschaft so beherrscht. Noch im Ehebett war Anna zwischen ihnen' (p. 161).

However, at the same time Hasler discreetly but persistently chips away at the traditional opposition of mistress and maid and re-figures them in such a way that increasingly Frau Tschudi comes to parallel Anna. In many ways they become equals – equals as *women*. In the words of Frau Zwicki, Anna's former employer: 'wenn man so lang und nah zusammenwohnet, da treten Unterschiede zurück, das Gemeinsame tritt herfür' (p. 48). The notion of 'das Gemeinsame' in this case is, I would suggest, the experience of sexual and economic oppression, the ruthless demands of labour in its two senses: the labour of childbirth and of menial service. Frau Tschudi, trapped in the demands of marital sex since the age of sixteen, has gone through ten pregnancies in so many years. The monotony of her existence – 'Schwangerwerden und Gebären' (p. 55) – echoes the 'Einerlei' (p. 36) of Anna's existence, the dreary sequence of some ten employers. In an eloquent passage, Frau Tschudi reflects on the constraints of her life – caught up in the dictates of 'müssen', she envies Anna for her relative freedom, the capacity of 'können': 'Die kann sich ohne Anhang bewegen, unsereiner muß auf Mann und Kinder Rücksicht nehmen. ... Unsereiner muß bei Tag und Nacht tun, was der Mann will, selbst im Bett' (p. 55). Again, Anna's fate figures as a parallel. Although she has only given birth twice, she is weary of the sexual game between master and maid, the 'Spiel mit den uralten Regeln' (p. 72). When Dr Tschudi attempts to enter Anna's bedroom, the narrative voice shifts into free indirect speech and conjoins patterns of sexual and religious 'Herrschaft' in a manner reminiscent of Jelinek's most provocative moments: 'Der Herr, gebeugt von Schuldgefühlen, schleicht sich zur Magd ... Und die Magd liegt da ... Sei stille dem Herrn und warte auf ihn, Psalm 37,7. Der Herr ist mit dir bei Tag und Nacht' (p. 73). Both mistress and servant are entrapped in socially circumscribed silence – both lack the language to articulate their claims to genuine subjectivity. Only one form of expression is given to them, and it is one beyond their control: giving birth. As Frau Tschudi puts it: 'Dieser Bauch, der sich immer wieder füllt, von neuem wölbt' (p. 56). The import of her comment extends, of course, to the collective of all those women who are burdened down by unwanted pregnancies. One thinks, for example, of Anna's sister, Barbara, who is a grandmother, yet finds herself pregnant again: 'Ihr Gesicht war spitz geworden, ... aber der Bauch, als hätte er Saft und Kraft aus dem Körper gezogen, wölbte sich unter der Schürze' (p. 105).

In sharpest contrast to French feminist theory as epitomized by Hélène Cixous, Hasler does not mythologize menstruation and childbirth into symbols of womanhood, but rather *politicizes* these motifs. At a number of key points, the narrative makes the link between private and public, between sexual and socio-political oppression. Crucially, Anna likens unspoken words to a monstrous pregnancy: 'Worte, die man nicht sagen kann, werden schwer und schwerer, Steinmüller! Bleiben im Bauch drin mit der Wut' (p. 82). In reply, he widens the metaphor and points to the pregnant silence of discontent amongst the masses: 'Das ist gefährlich, alle die vielen Mäuler, die Bäuche mit den ungesagten

Wörtern. Wörter, die man schluckt, werden lebendig, Anna. Wetten, die kommen in irgendeiner Form wieder heraus. Das erleben wir vielleicht noch, Anna, daß die Wörter, von gewaltigem Druck herausgeschleudert, selbständig durch die Luft fliegen' (p. 83). Steinmüller is clearly thinking of potential revolution, but his wording is crucial within the *metaphorical* nexus: it explicitly establishes the pattern of repression and expression, and in this sense it challenge us to re-think the recalcitrant figure of Anna Maria who spits pins and nails.

On the overt level of the novel, the girl is part of the 'Herrschaft' ranged against the servant and exerts her authority as the little mistress. Both the text and the postscript suggest that her fits are faked, that Anna Maria asserts herself and succeeds in becoming the centre of attention. There are, no doubt, several psychological explanations which one could bring to bear on her behaviour, but within the present context I am not concerned with the issue of causality. Rather, I want to stress that Anna Maria's action crucially interlinks with the meta-phorical and literal patterns of repression and expression: her spitting of pins and nails figures first and foremost as pure *ex-pression*. The nature of that expression is, of course, open to a wide spectrum of interpretations given the symbolic poly-valence of 'Stecknadeln' and 'Nägel' within our cultural system. Let me highlight three particular points.

Firstly, Anna Maria closely resembles her mother. The first image of Frau Tschudi stresses her 'verkniffene(n) Mund' (p. 12). The motif is later taken up and linked with the rigid figure of Anna Maria: 'starr, die Lippen zu einem Strich zusammengepreßt, jetzt sieht es der Mutter ähnlich' (p. 40). The mother's latent frustration reverberates in her daughter. In contrast to her elder sister, who excels at the art of 'Knicks hier, Knicks da' and 'artig lächeln' (p. 58), Anna Maria is fascinated by the uncanny, by images beyond the margin of normality. She consistently rebels against the constraints of socialisation. Her protest 'was ich nicht will, muß ich nicht' (p. 52) strikingly inverts her mother's lament on the dictates of 'müssen' and spits out discontent, as it were, in the form of pins and nails.

Secondly, Anna Maria's act of expression directly links with the pent-up anger and frustration of Anna Göldin, the girl's adoptive mother, and, crucially, with the silence of all those who have no voice of their own – in the words of Steinmüller the 'Bäuche mit den ungesagten Wörtern'

(p. 83). Swallowed words gain metamorphosed shape in the pins and nails – they 'kommen in irgendeiner Form wieder heraus' (p. 83). The link between Anna Maria's fits and the public realm is made explicit at the end of chapter 3, Part III. Here, Steinmüller holds that Anna Maria's fits are not an arbitrary phenomenon – 'nicht von ungefähr' – but articulate, in monstrously distorted form, the silenced discontent within the political, cultural system: 'Es wird mit solchen und ähnlichen Spukkereien noch ärger kommen. Solange nur wenige das Sagen haben, den übrigen der Mund verschlossen wird, werden die Nähkästen des Teufels weiterhin bemüht' (p. 149). Steinmüller's viewpoint is reinforced by the narrator's loosely connected metaphorical comment: 'Nicht nur im Darm mit seinen peristaltischen Zuckungen, auch anderswo sticht, zwickt und zwackt es, Stöcke schweben durch die Luft, Nadeln fliegen durch die Zimmer, das Kind hat Ohrensausen, vernimmt Stimmen …' (p. 149).

Thirdly, on a Freudian reading the pins and nails attain a double meaning. Within the overall context, their phallic shape conjures up images of women penetrated, pinned and nailed down by male sexual urge. They metaphorically interlink with the oppressive force of sexuality which plagues both Frau Tschudi and Anna Göldin. Anna Maria's fits are thus an integral part of the novel's reflections on 'Herrschaft'. In a wider sense, the spitting of pins may be seen as the rejection of a particular legacy – the culture of needlework which Freud ascribes to woman in compensation for her lack of a phallus. By virtue of such metaphorical associations, the text reaches back to countless female figures who have sewn or embroidered their way through the literary tradition. Within the novel itself it is tellingly enough Anna Maria's mother who, when we first see her, 'läßt Stickrahmen, farbige Garnfäden, Nadeln sinken' (p. 11).

As these interpretative possibilities suggest, Hasler manipulates the historically given object, the pins and nails, so as to achieve a maximum of metaphorical potency. The force of these poly-valent elements does not detract from the primary polemical concern of the novel – rather it enriches the text of protest by lending it the depth of a complex cultural argument, one which reflects on, and ultimately deconstructs, the traditional narrative of the witch and the possessed creature. The archivally validated event sequence is, by any standards, an impassioned indictment of mechanisms of 'Herrschaft'; but it is through the poly-valent symbols that the novel fully retraces and interrogates the nexus of gendered entrapment and extends the feminist argument to a powerful socio-political critique.

Bibliography

Eveline Hasler, *Novemberinsel – Erzählung*, 4th edition (Munich: dtv, 1993)
  Anna Göldin Letzte Hexe – Roman, 11th edition (Munich: dtv, 1995)
  Ibicaba – Das Paradies in den Köpfen – Roman, 6th edition (Munich: dtv, 1993)
  Der Riese im Baum – Roman (Munich: dtv, 1992)
Gertrud Leutenegger, *Das verlorene Monument* (Frankfurt am Main: Suhrkamp, 1985)
Maria Waser, *Die Geschichte der Anna Waser: Ein Roman aus der Wende des 17. Jahrhunderts* (Frauenfeld: Huber, 1959)
Andrea Wörle (ed), *Frauen in der Schweiz: Erzählungen*, 2nd edition (Munich: dtv, 1991)

Joy Charnley

Women Writing in French-speaking Switzerland

Early writers

Women in *Suisse romande* have a long, although often forgotten, history of writing and publishing going back as far as the sixteenth century, when women such as Jeanne de Jussie (1503–1561) and later Marie Huber (1695–1753) began to be active essentially as writers of religious treatises and religious-inspired poetry.[1] In the eighteenth century, Isabelle de Charrière (1740–1805), who was of Dutch origin, marked the move towards the writing of fiction with her epistolary novels, *Lettres neuchâteloises* (1784) and *Lettres écrites de Lausanne* (1785), in which she touches on such essential questions as women's position in society and their mistreatment by men. Similar themes were also taken up by Germaine de Staël (1766–1817) in novels such as *Delphine* (1802) and *Corinne* (1807). Like Isabelle de Charrière she established in Coppet a *salon* attended by well-known intellectuals and writers of the day, many of them, as she was, exiles from Napoleonic France. De Staël's early years in Paris and her life-long connection to the city have often led to her being considered a French writer, much like Rousseau and others, but she in fact spent a good part of her life in exile in Switzerland and through her intellectual activities there and her strong belief in the importance of a European vision, did much to establish the notion that an intellectual centre outside France was entirely viable.[2]

---

1   See Christiane Makward, 'Le récit féminin de Suisse: Un autre regard?' *Présence Francophone* 36 (1990), 7–33 (pp. 7–11).
2   Makward, pp. 10–11; Lucienne Mazenod and Ghislaine Schoeller, *Dictionnaire des femmes célèbres* (Paris: Laffont, 1992). On other women writers of the nineteenth century see Doris Jakubec, *Femmes écrivains suisses de langue française. Solitude surpeuplée* (Lausanne: Editions d'en bas, 1990), pp. 8–13.

Autobiography/women's issues

In the early twentieth century many women were given an opportunity to publish their first works by Albert Mermoud's *Guilde du Livre*,
founded in 1936, and amongst this first generation we find writers such
as Monique Saint-Hélier (1895–1959), Catherine Colomb (1899–1965),
Alice Rivaz (1901) and Corinna Bille (1912–1979).[3] It is perhaps indicative of the major role played by the *Guilde* in *Suisse romande* that it
facilitated the emergence of such a solid group of women writers at this
time, in contrast to German-speaking Switzerland, where it was not
until the mid-1970s that a comparable group began to emerge.

Although not overtly feminist, as later generations would be, the
works of Alice Rivaz turn around the often tiny detail of women's lives:
their working environment, their relationships with one another and
with men, their often problematic closeness to their mothers. Trapped
herself in a demanding job which prevented her from realising her full
potential as a writer before retirement, Rivaz powerfully evokes both
the working and private lives of secretaries in novels such as the ironi-
cally-titled *La paix des ruches* (1947). In this novel, considered by some
to be in some sense an early 'feminist' work, although not overtly so, the
narrator reflects on the fact that she no longer loves her husband and
contemplates divorce, whilst her colleagues, like her, ground down by
the pettiness and routine of office life, pursue love affairs or commit
suicide when love abandons them. The very moving *Comptez vos jours*
(1966) recounts a woman's oppressively close relationship with her age-
ing mother, and is clearly autobiographical. Rivaz does not however
concern herself exclusively or necessarily explicitly with women's lives,
as witnessed by her fine collection of short stories, *De mémoire et d'oubli*
(1973), in which both men and women face an unrelenting diet of
heartbreak, disappointment and tragedy. The little girl in 'Chante, Fanny'
learns to sing in order to placate her violent father, 'Le vieux militant'
dies disappointed and forgotten whilst the narrator of 'Mon fils ne le
permettra pas' listens to her neighbour recount his mother's inhuman

3 Doris Jakubec, 'The Swiss French Novel from 1945 to the Present', *Modern Swiss
   Literature. Unity and Diversity*, edited by John L. Flood (London: Wolff, 1985),
   pp. 57–69 (pp. 65–66).

treatment at the hands of doctors. An immense sadness permeates these stories, and the overwhelming impression is one of frustration, unsatisfied people living out their lives in quiet desperation.[4]

Women's lives and concerns, often grounded in autobiography, as with Rivaz, are central to the works of Yvette Z'Graggen (1920), whose career began in 1944 with *La vie attendait*. Through successive novels and short stories, *Chemins perdus* (1971), *Cornelia* (1985) and the more recent *La Punta* (1992), Z'Graggen explores a variety of themes: women's search for independence, their experiences (often disappointing or conflictual) within the couple, their often complicated and frequently unsuccessful relationships with their parents, their desire to raise their own children differently and create for them another type of society, a healthier environment.[5] Z'Graggen's heroines reflect closely her own life and experiences, developing from the uncertain twenty-something characters just starting out in life who figure in *L'Herbe d'octobre* (1950) and *Le filet de l'oiseleur* (1956) through to the older more assured heroine of *Un été sans histoire* (1962), experiencing a love affair with a younger man, and later still the narrator of *La Punta*, who retires to Spain with her husband, only to find that she is much more adventurous than him and can no longer contemplate the life of routine which he would like. In this last work, Z'Graggen also tackles the question of old age, the changing social expectations and the limiting stereotypes which are imposed on women.

This desire to have recourse to the 'je', described by Philippe Carrard as 'la forme spontanée et immédiate' for many women writers,[6] was considered 'omniprésent' by the writer Odette Renaud-Vernet (1932–1993) at the end of the seventies.[7] That particular decade saw the emergence of several women who, directly or indirectly, drew in their writing on their experience as women. Anne Cuneo (1936) in works such

---

4 On Rivaz see Roger-Louis Junod, *Alice Rivaz* (Editions Universitaires de Fribourg, 1980).

5 On Z'Graggen see *Ecriture*, 46 (Automne 1995) and Edith Habersaat, *Yvette Z'Graggen* (Editions Universitaires de Fribourg, 1987).

6 Philippe Carrard, 'Variations sur le "je": quelques aspects du récit homodiégétique dans la littérature contemporaine de Suisse romande', *Présence Francophone* 20 (printemps 1980), 163–178 (p. 164).

7 Odette Renaud-Vernet, 'Prosatrices romandes', *Magazine littéraire* 141 (octobre 1978), 91–92 (p. 92).

as *Gravé au diamant* (1967) or her two-volume autobiography, *Les portes du jour* (1980) and *Le temps des loups blancs* (1982) reveals her efforts as an Italian child to fit into Swiss society and her struggle to overcome discrimination against her both as a woman and as a 'foreigner.' Not fully accepted in Switzerland, and yet no longer completely at ease defining herself as 'Italian', Cuneo felt somewhat lost between the two identities and her unhappy experiences at a religious *pension* in Lausanne leave a profound impression on her, a strong desire to achieve more than the little that is expected of her. In *Zéro positif* (1975) Anne-Lise Grobéty's 'stream of consciousness' style traces a woman's breakdown, alcoholism and depression. Written, says Grobéty, with no 'intention féministe'[8], this novel indeed presents us with a heroine who is in crisis, but does not yet have a solution or any clear demands to make on society or her husband.[9]

In Monique Laederach's *La femme séparée* (1982), however, the heroine Anne has gone a stage further and is taking her first tentative steps towards independence. Treated like a child by her husband, Anne 'escapes' her marriage through another man, her lover, but gradually realises that she has exchanged one form of dependence for another and must seek a more profoundly autonomous way of life. In searching to regain her identity, lost during her years of marriage, Anne comes to understand that she must look inwards to herself, 'en elle-même', to find resources there, rather than continually seeking guidance from others.[10]

The 'autre voix' with which women speak[11] is particularly evident in the presence in their works of the female body: the pleasure it may experience, the illnesses or pain it may endure. Thus blood, periods, pregnancy, miscarriage and breast cancer figure largely in works such as *Zéro positif* and Cuneo's *Mortelle maladie* (1969) and *Une cuillerée de bleu* (1979). A woman's first experience of sex, disastrous and unsatisfying, is alluded to by Grobéty in *Infiniment plus* (1989) where she explores a

8 In David Bevan, *Ecrivains d'aujourd'hui. La littérature romande en vingt entretiens* (Lausanne: Editions 24 Heures, 1986), p. 87.

9 Carrard, pp. 172–174.

10 Neil B. Bishop, 'Féminitude suisse: l'œuvre poétique et romanesque de Monique Laederach', *Présence Francophone* 45 (1994), 117–132 (p. 124).

11 Monique Laederach, 'Littérature féminine', *Magazine littéraire* 161 (mai 1980), 67–68 (p. 68).

woman's realisation that she had never previously faced up to the reality of her own passions and desires. In *Un temps de colère et d'amour* (1980) Z'Graggen describes a young woman's doubts and fears before she first has sex, and then graphically details her terrified reaction to the haemorrhage which follows her loss of virginity. Grobéty also provides a less than idyllic vision of motherhood in her darkly sardonic 'Maternaire', a short story in the collection *La fiancée d'hiver* (1984), and in the work of non-fiction which she coauthored with Monique Laederach and Amélie Plume, *Littérature féminine ou féministe?*, she writes forcefully of the bar to female creativity which children represent.[12]

If the female body has become central for many women writers since the late sixties, there are still relatively few who have written about female sexuality as openly and frankly as Grisélidis Réal (1929). In *Le noir est une couleur* (1974) she recounts her life as a prostitute in Geneva and Germany, her attempts to keep both herself and her children whilst going through a series of relationships with black American soldiers (hence the title) and escaping from the clutches of assorted policemen, judges and social workers. Réal describes her desires, her fantasies, her experiences with men, both good and bad, and her ferocious need to be independent, free to live as she likes with no petty rules and conventions imposed by others. More recently, and in a different style, Amélie Plume (1943) has used humour to write not only about women's often disappointing or frustrating experiences of sex, but also their assertive expression of 'what they want.'

On the whole the generation of writers which includes Laederach (1938) and Grobéty (1949) is thus much more 'resolutely feminist' than earlier generations[13], and amongst both established writers and more recent arrivals such as Silvia Ricci-Lempen (1951) and Ursula Gaillard (1947) autobiography and the female self continue to be of central importance. However, another tendency can be perceived amongst some women writers, whose writing could perhaps be described as 'implicitement féministe'[14], that is to say they write about women without necessarily seeing it as their primary function to focus upon 'women's

12 Anne-Lise Grobéty, 'Du côté de l'écriture féminine ... ', *Littérature féminine ou féministe?* (Genève: Zoé, 1983) pp. 6–27 (pp. 9–13).
13 Jakubec p. 67.
14 Makward p. 27.

issues.' Others again appear to have completely changed direction: Anne
Cuneo for example, who in 1975 considered herself to be an 'écrivain
féministe'[15], but whose writing has now clearly moved away from what
has been described as 'la fiction gynocentrique engagée'[16] towards novels such as *Station Victoria* (1989). As Doris Jakubec has said of Amélie
Plume, increasingly in the nineties women writers seem to be turning
to other modes of expression, adopting new accents, feeling that times
have changed and that perhaps 'le temps de pleurer et de gémir sur notre
sort' is over.[17]

Social issues

Since the 1960s there has been a noticeable tendency for writers in
French-speaking Switzerland to be politically and socially less 'engagés'
than their counterparts in *Suisse alémanique*,[18] a tendency which writers such as Grobéty and Laederach, members of the Groupe d'Olten,
have themselves remarked upon.[19] If it is true that it is rare to see major social issues being tackled head-on in the contemporary literature
of *Suisse romande*, many are indirectly critical of the society in which
they live.

We have seen the quiet but forceful comment which Alice Rivaz
makes on the lives which people live and the lack of joy which she sees
around her. In her autobiographical novel *Un temps de colère et d'amour*
(1980), Yvette Z'Graggen also expresses a desire for a freer, more open,
less hypocritical society, often contrasting Switzerland with Italy and the

---

15 Anne Cuneo, 'Féminisme et écriture', *Arts et spectacles en Suisse romande*, 3 (18
   décembre 1975 – 7 janvier 1976), p. 8.
16 Makward, p. 27.
17 Doris Jakubec, *Solitude surpeuplée* (p. 19).
18 Yves Bridel, 'Y a-t-il une littérature romande aujourd'hui?', in *Vous avez dit
   'Suisse romande'?*, edited by René Knusel and Daniel Seiler (Lausanne: Insti-
   tut de Science politique, 1984) pp. 125–137 (p. 134); Yves Bridel, 'Quelques
   aspects de la littérature romande de 1945 à 1970', *Französisch Heute* (September
   1990), 219–223 (pp. 221–222); Manfred Gsteiger, *La nouvelle littérature romande*
   (Vevey: Galland, 1978) p. 194.
19 Bevan, p. 86 and p. 115.

very different atmosphere which she experiences there. She criticises Swiss society for being unable and unwilling to face up to unpleasant truths, preferring to pretend that illness and death do not exist or can be forgotten if hidden away. Similarly, Anne-Lise Grobéty's short story 'Défense d'entrer' (in *La fiancée d'hiver*) can easily be read as a critical comment upon that same society, in which people barricade themselves into their homes in their fear of the outside world. Although essentially a novel about a woman's gradual 'prise de conscience', Laederach's *La femme séparée* also provides comment upon 'l'univers suisse' of the 1970s: drugs, anti-nuclear protests, young people contesting the established order and seeking new ways of living.[20]

More explicitly, racism is the central theme in Anne Cuneo's *La vermine* (1970) in which Italian immigrants all over Switzerland return to their homeland *en masse*, the economy collapses and lurking prejudices are revealed. Injustice, discrimination and social class emerge once again in her *Piano du pauvre* (1975), a sympathetic portrait of accordion-player Denise Letourneur. In works such as *La Malvivante* (1978) and *La Pérégrine* (1983) Mireille Kuttel (1928), herself of Italian descent, also tackles the theme of Italian immigrants, particularly women, facing problems of integration in Switzerland.

War and its impact on human beings preoccupies several writers: Laederach again in *Trop petits pour Dieu* (1986), Agota Kristof (1935) who pursues her investigation of truth and identity in *Le grand cahier* (1986), *La preuve* (1988) and *Le troisième mensonge* (1991) or Yvette Z'Graggen who adopts a more personal approach in *Les années silencieuses* (1982). She retraces the war years in Switzerland by using a combination of the diary which she kept at the time, history books and newspaper reports for the years in question. Her investigation leads her to the honest but painful conclusion that although manifestly ill-informed by the newspapers, she, like many other Swiss, was doubtlessly guilty of not really wanting to know the truth about what was happening to the Jews, and was perfectly happy to continue to consider Switzerland as a haven for escaping refugees.

20 Bevan, p. 116.

Other paths

Many women writers born around the turn of the century encountered
problems with being recognised, either because their style and the lib-
erties they took with form gained them a reputation as 'difficult' writers (as was the case with Catherine Colomb who in a sense prefigures
the *nouveau roman*), or because they were categorised with a safe, limiting label, like Corinna Bille, for a long time dubbed a 'regional writer.'[21]
Although it is clear that Bille and her husband Maurice Chappaz (1916)
came to be very closely identified with the Valais and could be seen as
part of the movement away from 'l'engagement social' and towards the
region,[22] and although Bille does indeed bring alive for us this region
in which she lived for so many years, she also does much more. In works
such as *La fraise noire* (1968) she brings the fantastic into the everyday
world with her ghostly figures, her tales of death and suicide ('Le café
des voyageurs'), her stories of impossible or lost love ('Ma forêt, mon
fleuve', 'Un amant qui n'a pas existé') and her marvellous evocation of
nature. Like Colomb, she brought a new tone and style to writing in
Suisse romande.

Other worlds were physically explored by women travellers, who like
well-known Swiss men (Blaise Cendrars, Nicolas Bouvier) feel the need
to reach beyond the narrow confines of Switzerland, perhaps as Barilier
says in some way seeking their own identity through this form of 'mon-
dialisme'.[23] In the late nineteenth century already, Isabelle Eberhardt
(1877–1904), of Russian origin and a convert to Islam, travelled through
North Africa and recounted her adventures in works which were published posthumously (*Notes de route*, 1908, *Dans l'ombre chaude de l'Islam*,
1921). From the 1930s onwards Ella Maillart (1903–1997) travelled to

21 Jakubec, *Solitude surpeuplée*, p. 15.
22 Bridel, 'Quelques aspects de la littérature romande de 1945 à 1990', p. 222;
   Monique Moser-Verrey, 'La littérature romande et ses contextes', *Etudes Fran-
   çaises*, 28, 1 (1992), 173–188 (p. 181). Roger Francillon reminds us of Chappaz'
   courageous position with regard to economic and tourist developments in the
   Valais, evidence of a certain 'engagement' – see 'Dans le sérail helvétique. Le
   guerrier, l'ivrogne, le berger et l'eunuque', *Filiations et filatures. Littérature et critique en Suisse romande* (Genève: Zoé, 1991), pp. 11–88 (p. 78).
23 Etienne Barilier, 'Littérature romande', *Etudes de Lettres*, 4 (1982), 1–14 (p. 4, p. 7).

countries which few Westerners (particularly Western women) had ever seen, publishing her accounts of Russia (*Parmi la jeunesse russe*, 1932), China (*Oasis interdites*, 1937) and her journey through the Middle East to Afghanistan with Annemarie Schwarzenbach (*La voie cruelle*, 1952 – first published in English in 1947, like *Gypsy afloat* which appeared in 1942).[24] Maillart travelled partly as a reaction against society, attempting to escape from what she has called 'notre civilisation de fous ... cette vie que je détestais',[25] and partly in search of answers to her questions and doubts, as she puts it, 'pourquoi on vit.'

In the 1980s and 1990s this tradition of the *récit de voyage* has been continued by writers and travellers such as Laurence Déonna (1937) who has taken a particular interest in the Middle East and the lives of Muslim women, and clearly displays her feminist standpoint in works such as *Yémen* (1983) and *Syriens, Syriennes 1992–1994* (1995). Such women make an important contribution to travel writing, and in their desire to discover and recount other nations, other cultures, they remind us of the many generations of Swiss who have travelled and explored.

Conclusion

As we have seen, women have been a presence in *Suisse romande* literature for several centuries, bringing their own distinctive voice to that corner of the francophone world. Since the Second World War, however, they have come much more to the fore, aided by improved publication prospects and changing social attitudes and perhaps encouraged by the success of earlier generations. Women writers have played a major role in revitalising literature in French-speaking Switzerland, giving voice to themes and thoughts which had not previously been central

---

24 Annemarie Schwarzenbach (1908–1942), a member of the famous Wille family, was a rather depressive woman who had a serious drug problem. This unfortunately gave rise to some tension between her and Maillart during their journey. Schwarzenbach subsequently wrote a book entitled *Das glückliche Tal* (1940), translated into French by Yvette Z'Graggen and published as *La Vallée heureuse* (Lausanne: Aire, 1991).

25 Interview in *Le Nouveau Quotidien* (16 août 1992), pp. 3–4 (p. 4).

and adopting approaches (such as interior monologue or the stream of consciousness) which initially often surprised or displeased.

Anne-Lise Grobéty is quite clear about the importance of the emergence of women writers, not just for women but also for men and society at large. All must ultimately benefit from this other voice and the different tones which it can bring to literature[26] and it is now obvious that the days when a critic dared to describe a woman's novel as 'un roman de femme écrit avec une rigueur d'homme'[27] are long gone. One important example of these new directions and tones is found in the humour which is the hallmark of writers such as Amélie Plume who, in works like *Les aventures de Plumette et de son premier amant* (1981) and *Oui Emile pour la vie* (1984), charts the development of a relationship, the mistakes, the potential pitfalls. In *Hélas, nos chéris sont nos ennemis* (1995) she brings together an orchestra of women's voices, complaining, rejoicing, lamenting, comparing, recounting their lives and their adventures. The light, joyful tone here is new, marking a move away from the 'littérature triste, qui sourit rarement'[28] to which the literature of *Suisse romande* has been likened. In this, as in so much else, women writers are showing the way and marking out new paths for future generations, represented by younger writers such as Laurence Chauvy (1959), Patricia Hernandez (1972) and Anne-Lise Thurler (1960), whose works, tackling themes ranging from madness to African refugees in Switzerland, will take literature in *Suisse romande* through to the twenty-first century.

---

26 Anne-Lise Grobéty, *Littérature féminine ou féministe?*, pp. 26–27.
27 J. R. Fiechter, describing Yvette Z'Graggen's *Le filet de l'oiseleur* in *Cahiers de l'Alliance Cuturelle romande*, 14 (novembre 1969), 62–68 (p. 62).
28 AugusteViatte, *Histoire comparée des littératures francophones* (Paris: Nathan, 1980), p. 167.

Bibliography

General works

Jean-Pierre Beaumarchais, Daniel Couty, Alain Rey (eds.), *Dictionnaire des littératures de langue française*, 4 vols (Paris: Bordas, 1994)

Yves Bridel, Adrien Pasquali, *Théâtres d'écritures. Comment travaillent les écrivains?* *Enquête auprès d'écrivains suisses* (Berne: Lang, 1993)

Christophe Calame, *Sept cents ans de littérature en Suisse romande* (Paris: Editions de la Différence, 1991)

Henri-Charles Dahlem, *Sur les pas d'un lecteur heureux. Guide littéraire de la Suisse* (Lausanne: Aire, 1991)

Henri-Charles Dahlem, Alain Nicollier, *Dictionnaire des écrivains suisses d'expression française*, 2 vols (Genève: Editions GVA, 1994)

Gérard Froidevaux, *Ecrivains de Suisse romande* (Zug: Klett und Balmer, 1990)

Bertil Galland, *La littérature de la Suisse romande expliquée en un quart d'heure* (Genève: Zoé, 1986), pp. 9–36

Franck Jotterand, *Pourquoi j'écris* (La Gazette Littéraire, 1971)

Manfred Gsteiger, *La nouvelle littérature romande* (Vevey: Galland, 1978)

Pierre-Olivier Walzer, *Dictionnaire des littératures suisses* (Lausanne: Aire, 1991)

Critical works

Georges Anex, *L'arrache-plume. Chroniques de littérature romande 1965–1980* (Lausanne: Aire, 1980)

Peter André Bloch (ed.), *La Licorne. La Suisse romande et sa littérature* (Publications de l'UFR de langues et littératures de Poitiers, 1989)

Mousse Boulanger, Henri Corbat, *Littératures de Suisse romande* (Saved S.A., 1988)

Jacques Chessex, 'Blessures d'Anne-Lise Grobéty', *Les Saintes Ecritures* (Lausanne: Galland, 1972), pp. 189–192

Anne Cuneo, 'Intellectuel excessif s'abstenir?', *Ecriture*, 37 (Printemps 1991), 61–71

Béatrice Didier, *L'écriture-femme* (Paris: PUF, 1981)

Ecriture, 33 (Automne 1989). Special Issue on Bille.

Ecriture, 47 (Printemps 1996). Dossier on Réal.

Etudes de Lettres, 3 (Automne 1995). Special Issue on Monique Saint-Hélier.

Françoise Fornerod, 'Yvette Z'Graggen: de la fiction à la vérité', *Bulletin francophone de la Finlande*, 4 (1992), 76–82

Edith Habersaat, *Yvette Z'Graggen* (Editions Universitaires de Fribourg, 1987)

Monique Moser-Verrey, 'La mémoire de l'histoire chez quelques écrivaines romandes des années 80', *Présence Francophone*, 41 (1992), 97–113

Quarto, 6 (décembre 1995). Special Issue on Bille.

Literary works

Corinna Bille, *La fraise noire* (Lausanne: Guilde du Livre, 1968)

La demoiselle sauvage (Vevey: Galland, 1974)

Douleurs paysannes (Lausanne: Guilde du Livre, 1953)

Laurence Chauvy, *La montagne* (Lausanne: Aire, 1989)

Catherine Colomb, *Châteaux en enfance* (Lausanne: Guilde du Livre, 1945, re-edited Lausanne: Rencontre/Aire, 1968 and L'Age d'Homme, 1983)

> *Les esprits de la terre* (Lausanne: Rencontre, 1953, re-edited Bibliothèque romande, 1972)

> *Œuvres complètes* (Lausanne: L'Age d'Homme, 1993)

Anne Cuneo, *Gravé au diamant* (Lausanne: Aire, 1967)

> *Mortelle maladie* (Lausanne: Aire, 1969)

> *Une cuillerée de bleu* (Vevey: Galland, 1979)

> *Le piano du pauvre* (Vevey: Galland, 1975)

> *Les portes du jour* (Vevey: Galland, 1980)

> *Le temps des loups blancs* (Vevey: Galland, 1982)

Laurence Déonna, *Syriens, Syriennes 1992–1994* (Genève: Zoé, 1995)

> *Yémen* (Paris: Arthaud, 1983)

Marie-Claire Dewarrat, *L'eté sauvage* (Lausanne: Aire, 1985)

Ursula Gaillard, *Paysage arrêté* (Lausanne: Editions d'en bas, 1986)

Anne-Lise Grobéty, *La fiancée d'hiver* (Lausanne: Editions 24 Heures, 1984)

> *Infiniment plus* (Yvonand: Campiche, 1989)

> *Pour mourir en février* (Lausanne: Cahiers de la Renaissance Vaudoise 1970, re-edited Lausanne: Editions 24 Heures, 1984)

> *Zéro positif* (Vevey: Galland, 1975, re-edited Lausanne: 24 Heures, 1984)

Patricia Hernandez, *Contes fous aux portes de la mort* (Lausanne: Editions d'en bas, 1990)

Agota Kristof, *Le grand cahier* (Paris: Seuil, 1986)

> *La preuve* (Paris: Seuil, 1988)

> *Le troisième mensonge* (Paris: Seuil, 1991)

Mireille Kuttel, *La Pérégrine* (Lausanne: L'Age d'Homme, 1983)

Monique Laederach, *J'ai rêvé Lara debout* (Genève: Zoé, 1990)

> *La femme séparée* (Lausanne: Aire, 1982, re-edited Lausanne: L'Age d'Homme, 1993)

> *Trop petits pour Dieu* (Lausanne: Aire, 1986)

Ella Maillart, *La voie cruelle* (Genève: Jeheber, 1952, re-edited Paris: Payot, 1989)

> *Parmi la jeunesse russe* (Paris: Fasquelle, 1932, re-edited Lausanne: Editions 24 Heures, 1989)

> *Oasis interdites* (Paris: Grasset, 1937, re-edited Paris: Payot, 1984)

Rose-Marie Pagnard, *Séduire, dit-elle* (Lausanne: Aire, 1985)

Marie-José Piguet, *Reviens ma douce* (Lausanne: Galland, 1974, re-edited Lausanne: Aire, 1989)

Amélie Plume, *Les aventures de Plumette et de son premier amant* (Genève: Zoé, 1981)

> *Oui Emile pour la vie* (Genève: Zoé, 1984)

> *Promenade avec Emile L* (Genève: Zoé, 1992)

> *Hélas nos chéris sont nos ennemis* (Genève: Zoé, 1995)

Grisélidis Réal, *Le noir est une couleur* (Paris: Balland, 1974, re-edited Lausanne: Editions d'en bas, 1989).

Odette Renaud-Vernet, *Les Temps forts* (Lausanne: Aire, 1974).

Silvia Ricci-Lempen, *Le sentier des éléphants* (Lausanne: Aire, 1996).

Un homme tragique (Lausanne: Aire, 1991).

Alice Rivaz, *Comptez vos jours* (Paris: Corti, 1966, re-edited Lausanne: L'Age d'Homme, 1984)

De mémoire et d'oubli (Lausanne: Rencontre-Aire, 1973, re-edited Lausanne: Aire, 1992)

La paix des ruches (Paris: LUF, 1947, re-edited Lausanne: L'Age d'Homme, 1984)

Catherine Safonoff, *Retour, retour* (Genève: Zoé, 1984)

Monique Saint-Hélier, *Bois mort* (Paris: Grasset, 1934, re-edited Lausanne: L'Age d'Homme, 1985)

Le martin-pêcheur (Paris: Grasset, 1953, re-edited Lausanne: L'Age d'Homme, 1987)

Anne-Lise Thurler, *Le crocodile ne dévore pas le pangolin* (Genève: Zoé, 1996)

Yvette Z'Graggen, *Chemins perdus* (Lausanne: Aire, 1971)

Cornelia (Lausanne: Aire, 1985)

Un été sans histoire (Neuchâtel: La Baconnière, 1962, re-edited Lausanne: Aire, 1987)

Le filet de l'oiseleur (Genève: Jeheber, 1956, re-edited Lausanne: Aire, 1988)

L'herbe d'octobre (Genève: Jeheber, 1950, re-edited Lausanne: Aire, 1989)

La punta (Lausanne: Aire, 1992)

Un temps de colère et d'amour (Lausanne: Aire, 1980, re-edited Lausanne: Aire, 1987)

Andrew Wilkin

New Women's Writing
in Italian-speaking Switzerland

In his critical anthology *Svizzera Italiana*, the Ticinese novelist and poet
Giovanni Orelli averred that 'one must say that a decisive and original
contribution has come to Ticinese narrative writing in recent years from
a few women writers who have been courageously involved in the literary quest'.[1] He cites in particular Alice Ceresa, Anna Felder, Fleur
Jaeggy and Elda Guidinetti. In similar vein, Bernhard Wenger, in his slim
volume *Le quattro letterature della Svizzera*, draws special attention to
Ceresa and Felder as having found their place 'in the literary and linguistic experimentalism' of new Swiss-Italian literature.[2]
    Whilst it is true that Swiss-Italian women writers are relatively few
in number (just like their male counterparts), it is equally the case that
they have featured consistently in the history of Swiss-Italian literature
since the moment in 1803 when Ticino and the Grigioni became sovereign cantons of Switzerland. It is, however, in the age dominated by
Francesco Chiesa (1871–1973), the acknowledged 'father figure' of
modern Swiss-Italian literature, that women writers began to make
their particular mark, in the 'new season of Swiss-Italian culture which,
after the almost exclusively political interests of the 19th century, turned
to literature, with a precise awareness of its own worth and of the values which were to be reclaimed and defended'.[3] Among such women

---

1 Giovanni Orelli, *Svizzera Italiana* (Brescia: Editrice La Scuola, 'Letteratura delle
   regioni d'Italia: Storia e testi', 1986), p. 28. Translations into English of cita-
   tions, here and throughout this chapter, are by the present contributor.
2 Bernhard Wenger, *Le quattro letterature della Svizzera* (Zürich: Fondazione svizzera
   per la cultura Pro Helvetia, 'Quaderni d'informazione', 1985), p. 72. It is worthy of note that the translation into Italian of Wenger's text, originally published
   in German as *Die vier Literaturen der Schweiz*, with Giovanni Orelli as one his
   collaborators, was done by Alice Ceresa.
3 The citation is taken from the Ticinese critic Pio Fontana, who is quoted by
   Giovanni Orelli, *Svizzera Italiana*, op. cit., p. 20.

writers a position of particular prominence belongs to the dialect poet Alina Borioli (1887–1965)[4] as well as to her contemporary, the diaristic prose writer Maria Boschetti Alberti (1884–1951).[5] Together with Borioli and Boschetti Alberti, it would also be proper to make brief mention of the names of other women of the literary world who have made their mark in varying fields and *genres*. These include the poet Silvana Lattmann (born Neapolitan, but a Swiss citizen by marriage), the lexicographer Rosanna Zeli, the poet Giulietta Martelli-Tamoni (born 1889 in Buenos Aires, but a lifelong resident of the Italophone Val Mesolcina in the Grigioni, where she died in 1976), the younger prose-writers Anna Mosca, Elena Bonzanigo and Elena Rimoldi, the literary scholars Maria Teresa Casella and Carmela Colombo, and the former director of the Biblioteca Cantonale Adriana Ramelli.

As with their male counterparts, all of these women writers, irrespective of their principal *genre*, have had to face the paradoxical status of being a 'writer from Italian-speaking Switzerland who risks passing, in Milan, as a Swiss who has been *translated* into Italian by herself, whilst in Zürich they are like Italians who *must* be translated into German'.[6] Just like the 'father figure' Francesco Chiesa, they have all had to confront the 'potential obliteration of their own past which strikes more forcefully the peripheral regions of Switzerland, which are more exposed to being overwhelmed by the hegemonic, imported and consumer-led cultures [of their immediate neighbours]'.[7] Attention has been appropriately drawn to the simple statistical fact that mother-tongue Italophones account for just under 10 per cent of the resident population in Switzerland – some 622,000 persons – and that of these rather fewer

4 For Alina Borioli, see especially her dialect poem 'Ava Giuana' in the volume *Vos det la faura*, (Lugano: Edizione del Cantonetto, 1964). See also her collection of fables, legends and popular traditions, *La vecchia Leventina* (Bellinzona: Leins-Vescovi, 1926), which has been issued in a second revised edition (Lugano: Edizione del Cantonetto, 1973).
5 For Maria Boschetti Alberti, see especially *Il diario di Muzzano*, which stops (incomplete) at 8 May 1920, and her other prose work *La scuola serena di Agno*, first published in the journal *Adula*, 1926–27. The two works have subsequently been re-published and reprinted on several occasions by Editrice La Scuola of Brescia.
6 This acute observation was made by Giovanni Orelli in the dust-jacket notes to his volume *Svizzera Italiana, op. cit.*
7 ibid., p. 22.

than 242,000 (barely 39 per cent) are Swiss nationals.[8] In the rather stark terms of the literary 'market-place', therefore, Swiss–Italian literature, strictly construed, can be perceived in its untranslated form both as being generated by an internal minority for a domestic majority, *and* as having a sort of geo-linguistically associated export market as its potential prime outlet. This explains the somewhat Janus-like face of Swiss–Italian literary production, looking *in dentro* (as Ticinese Italian expresses it) to the Switzerland of Zürich and Bern, and at the same time *fuori* to its immediate cousin over the political border in Italy.[9] It has been, and is, an inescapable truism that Swiss–Italian literary production is inextricably intertwined with Italian–Italian literary production, and that – as such – the native Swiss–Italian product is considered by many to be a *regional* literature of Italy (in a rather similar fashion to the way in which Scottish literature often finds itself treated as a sub-species of English literature). It must be firmly noted, however, that confederal Switzerland has done much – particularly through the agency of Pro Helvetia – to confront and respond to the question of linguistic and cultural sovereignty in its several parts, especially by ensuring that meritorious works, irrespective of their regional linguistic origin, are translated and disseminated throughout the whole of Switzerland.

Where, then, do the key women Swiss–Italian prose writers of the modern age stand in this panoply of limitations? Certainly – and again like their male counterparts – they commonly have other gainful employment apart from their literary activity. Indeed, Giovanni Orelli once playfully (but realistically) stated that 'almost all Swiss–Italian writers are "Sunday morning writers" and especially in the months of July and August'.[10] Moreover, as Antonio Stäuble observed, 'there are various good publishers in Italian Switzerland, but none can compete with the

---

8 Bernhard Wenger, *Le quattro letterature della Svizzera,* op. cit., p. 7.
9 For a fuller treatment of the problem of the 'market' for Swiss-Italian literary production see Andrew Wilkin, 'In margine al rinnovamento della narrativa svizzero-italiana dal 1945 ad oggi', in *Gli spazi della diversità,* ed. by S.Vanvolsem, F. Musarra, and B.Van den Bossche (Rome: Bulzoni Editore; Leuven: Leuven University Press, 1995), pp. 531–543.
10 Giovanni Orelli, 'La posizione ambigua dello scrittore nella Svizzera italiana', in *Literatur aus der Schweiz: Texte und Materialien,* ed. by E. Amann and E. Faes (Zürich: Suhrkamp Verlag, 1978), pp. 476–482.

Italian houses for publicity and the distribution network; access to Italian publishers is difficult for a Swiss, even if s/he writes in Italian; the few who succeed [...] can be regarded as privileged'.[11] That privileged position has certainly been meritoriously achieved by Alice Ceresa, Fleur Jaeggy and Anna Felder, and in variant fashion by Elda Guidinetti.

Alice Ceresa was born in Basel in 1923 of parents from the GrigioneseVal Mesolcina, but for many years now (indeed since 1950) has been a resident of Rome. In the immediate post-war period she served as a journalist for Swiss-Italian affairs with the newspaper *Die Weltwoche*. She came to literary prominence in 1967 with the publication of her experimental avant-garde novel *La figlia prodiga*,[12] which was published by Einaudi and won her the Premio Viareggio for a First Work. With this work – which Ceresa wrote such that 'it would be analysed as in a laboratory' and '*not* for the pleasure of the so-called ordinary reader' – Einaudi launched a new series of books under the banner of 'Literary research: Italian series'. Ceresa herself said of *La figlia prodiga* (the title of which is a clear derivative of the Biblical prodigal son) that it was 'a novel so credible as to seem unreal: adventures lived anywhere by anyone, which fact simply attenuates its deadliness'. Professor Maria Corti, reviewing *La figlia prodiga*, opened by noting that

> there are those who look at trees in blossom in order to write a botanical tract and those who observe men who live and die in order to write a tract on the vices and virtues of men; but then there is also Alice Ceresa who contemplates hypothetical parents and a hypothetical prodigal daughter in order to extract from an abstract complex of possible situations her tract on the prodigality of the prodigal daughter; the matter of this book, therefore, resolves itself into an abstract squared.[13]

In parallel with her resumed journalistic (and subsequently also editorial) activities, Alice Ceresa has written a *racconto* entitled *La morte del padre* (1979) and a second novel *Bambine* (1990).[14] This latter novel

---

11 See Antonio Stäuble, 'Italian-Swiss Literature since the Second World War', in *Modern Swiss Literature. Unity and Diversity*, ed. by J. L. Flood (London: Oswald Wolff/Institute of Germanic Studies, 1985), pp. 19–33.

12 Alice Ceresa, *La figlia prodiga* (Turin: Einaudi, 1967).

13 Maria Corti, in *Strumenti critici*, 1967.

14 Alice Ceresa, 'La morte del padre', in *Nuovi argomenti*, 62 (aprile-giugno 1979), 69–92. – *Bambine* (Turin: Einaudi, 'Nuovi Coralli, 423', 1990).

undertakes a detailed, indeed meticulous, observation of the growing-up process of two young girls. This may appear, superficially, to mark a return to everyday novelistic normality, but the converse is true, because Ceresa shows how fear and horror can reside within the banality of daily existence, so that even tiny details, such as the description of their father's nose, his feet, or his severe glance, are capable of arousing either fear or jealousy. Alice Ceresa has also brought her experience as a writer to the collateral activity of translation: of particular note is her translation into Italian of the linguistically challenging novel *The incredible story of Johann the Good* by the Zürich-based writer Gerold Späth.

Whilst it is demonstrably the case that Ticinese culture has an evident direct linkage with the mainstream of Italian culture, it is also true that Ticinese culture has always endeavoured to keep itself separate out of a wish not to be entirely swamped or 'deformed' by the mass culture on its southern frontier. This is why certain Ticinese writers have in fact made a point of confirming their 'Swissness' by involving themselves personally in 'inner' Switzerland. Anna Felder, born in Lugano (1937), is a case in point. After gaining her high school *maturità*, she enrolled – unlike the many Italophone students who gravitate naturally to higher education in Italy – the Faculty of Arts at the University of Zürich, where she specialised in Romance languages. Following a period of study residence in Paris, she completed her degree at Zürich with a thesis on the work of the Nobel prize-winning Italian poet Eugenio Montale. The quality of this study was such that it was adjudged worthy of publication.[15]

Felder lives and works – she teaches Italian at the local high school – at Aarau, at the industrial crossroads of Switzerland, where once many immigrant Italian workers found employment. The lives of these Italian *Gastarbeiter* underpin her first narrative work, *Tra dove piove e non piove*.[16] Her second work, *La disdetta*, which was published in 1974 to much critical acclaim, with the major Italian novelist Italo Calvino numbering

---

15 Anna Felder, *La maschera di Montale* (Lugano: Arti Grafiche Gaggini-Bizzozero, 1968).

16 Anna Felder, *Tra dove piove e non piove* (Locarno: Pedrazzini, 1972). Interestingly, this work appeared chronologically first in German as *Quasi Heimweh* (Zürich: Rodana, 1970).

among its proponents, won her the Premio Schiller of 1975.[17] In it, Felder
considers the effects of a compulsory eviction order on a Lugano family
through the eyes of the household cat, who witnesses thereby the crum-
bling of a whole domestic world. Felder's collateral artistic involvement
as a writer of radio dramas has provided another outlet for her acute
observational skills. One should instance in this connection works for
Radio Zürich and Radio della Svizzera Italiana such as *Eva o l'esercizio
di pensiero* and *Tête-à-tête*. Her next narrative work, *Nozze alte*, appeared
in 1981.[18] It presents a modern reinterpretation of the Ovidian myth of
Philemon and his wife Baucis, who offered hospitality to the disguised
Zeus and Hermes, and is thus an addition to modern awareness of this
myth, which has been translated by both La Fontaine and Dryden, and
depicted by both Rubens and Rembrandt. Felder's more recent volume
of fiction, *Gli stretti congiunti*, – and here her work has frequently been
instanced as a re-evocation of Katherine Mansfield – is a collection of
fourteen *racconti* which were first written for a cycle of broadcasts on
Radio della Svizzera Italiana.[19] These tales are presented as an anthologi-
cal collection, but can also be read in sequence as if they were chapters
in a novel. They epitomise Felder's straightforward approach to narrative
writing: write simply about simple things. Thus the protagonists of the
individual tales – the wife, the husband, the mother, the father, the uncle, the grandfather, the lover, and so on – could each give a hand to another of the group, not because they are blood relatives (they are not), but
because they have been 'convened' by the author to form a sort of im-
provised 'ring-a-ring-o'-roses'. Yet each seems impatient to break the
chain, to escape out of his or her tale, not to be talked about any more.
Instead, each would prefer to 'escape back' within the four walls of his or
her own home and to accept and tolerate their 'normal' role, within the
real family, with all its domestic 'difficulties', but receptive of its comforting
support.

If it is broadly true that Swiss-Italian writers tend to be literary *ama-
teurs* who, because of the numerical circumscription of their natural
'market', frequently derive their principal income not from their literary

17 Anna Felder, *La disdetta* (Turin: Einaudi, 1974).
18 Anna Felder, *Nozze alte* (Locarno: Pedrazzini, 'Il pardo, 5', 1981).
19 Anna Felder, *Gli stretti congiunti* (Locarno: Pedrazzini, 'Il pardo, 6', 1982).

endeavours, but from other professional activities (most notably teaching), then Fleur Jaeggy is perhaps the exception who proves the rule. Jaeggy, who has always been careful not to declare her year of birth publicly, was born in Zürich of a family whose roots are in Locarno. She is now a long-time resident of Milan, and is a professional author who writes all her literary production in Italian. She composes her *racconti* 'assembled like sophisticated seismographs in order to seize, between the folds of life of her lightly-drawn characters, intimate secrets which those who do not turn and look pass over'.[20]

Of Fleur Jaeggy's first narrative work, *Il dito in bocca*, the Austrian writer Ingeborg Bachmann said 'in it the author has an enviable first glance at people and things, in her there is a mixture of relaxed lightness and authoritative wisdom',[21] whilst her next work, *L'angelo custode*, presents Jaeggy 'oscillating in her writing between miniaturised prose (which pleased critics such as Giorgio Manganelli) and tight dialogue' which can be found even in the epistolary passages.[22] One symptomatic excerpt reads as follows:

> I could tell you so many things about myself in general. The trouble is that I haven't got time to talk about them as a man is already blocking my path. He stops me, so I start walking faster. I reflect for a moment and then immediately ask myself if it wouldn't be better to turn round. Once upon a time, I met men at friends' houses, or at the homes of sons whose parents knew other parents and so on. Nowadays it is different. But never, I swear, would I stop long with such men. [...] As I quicken my step there are a thousand contradictions in me. It is these men, the ones who make me hesitate. It only needs one of them to give me a little push in the back and that moment, in which I wonder about turning back or not, has gone. That's how my life goes on.[23]

20 Giovanni Orelli, *Svizzera Italiana*, op. cit., p. 250.

21 Fleur Jaeggy, *Il dito in bocca* (Milan: Adelphi, 1968). Ingeborg Bachmann's assessment is reported both in the dust-jacket notes to *I beati anni del castigo*, q.v. below, and by Giovanni Orelli, *Svizzera Italiana*, op. cit., p. 250.

22 Fleur Jaeggy, *L'angelo custode* (Milan: Adelphi, 1971). The critical assessment is again from Giovanni Orelli, *Svizzera Italiana*, op. cit., p. 250.

23 This excerpt is drawn from an illustrative passage from Jaeggy's work discussed by Giovanni Orelli in 'Letteratura nella Svizzera Italiana, oggi. La narrativa', itself one of a cycle of sixteen lectures organised by the Associazione Cultura Popolare di Balerna between December 1981 and June 1982 and published as *Per conoscere la Svizzera Italiana* (Lugano: Edizioni Fondazione Pellegrini-Canevascini, 1985).

Following *Le statue d'acqua*,[24] Jaeggy came to genuinely well-merited attention with *I beati anni del castigo*, which won her the Premio Bagutta
of 1990.[25] This tale is set in a girls' boarding school in Appenzell in Switzerland. The atmosphere is both idyllic and yet wicked. A new girl ar-
rives: she is beautiful yet severe, perfect, she gives the impression of having
lived through everything already. The protagonist – another resident of
the school – feels attracted to this newly-arrived figure, who gives glimpses
of something which is quietly terrifying. The terrifying dimension reveals itself little by little: she is no-one's territory somewhere between
perfection and madness. 'And yet,' thinks the protagonist, 'these were the
best years – the years of punishment.' The style is clear and yet nervy. The
character notations are sharp, the intensity acute. The reader is left touched
by emotion, disconcerted, attracted and yet fearful. Joseph Brodsky observed of *I beati anni del castigo*: 'Reading time: about four hours. Dura-
tion of the memory, as for the writer: the rest of one's life'.[26] Of a partially different order, perhaps, is *La paura del cielo*.[27] This volume is a collection of seven stories, fast-moving, and written in a spare terse style.
They are typical of the 'calm experimentation' of Jaeggy.[28] And yet again
we find a thin veil of the terrifying (as in *I beati anni del castigo*); again we
have a sense of the illusory. In sequence the seven stories are: 'Senza
destino', 'Una moglie', 'La casa gratuita', 'La promessa', 'Porzia', 'I gemelli'
and 'La vecchia vanesia'. Over the years the works of Fleur Jaeggy have
become well known, have been translated into several languages, and 'have
been crowned with wide public and critical success'.[29]

---

24 Fleur Jaeggy, *Le statue d'acqua* (Milan: Adelphi, 1980). This text subsequently
   appeared in 1986 in German under the title of *Wasserstatuen*.
25 Fleur Jaeggy, *I beati anni del castigo* (Milan: Adelphi, 'Fabula, 33', 1989; 5th edition, 1990). This text also subsequently appeared in German, in 1996, under
   the title of *Die seligen Jahre der Züchtigung*.
26 This critical observation is reported on the dust-jacket of *La paura del cielo*, q.v.
   below.
27 Fleur Jaeggy, *La paura del cielo* (Milan: Adelphi, 'Fabula, 81', 1994).
28 This assessment of Jaeggy's work is made – with more particular reference to
   her earlier works – by Pietro Gibellini in the chapter 'Il Cerchio e la Retta:
   uno sguardo alla letteratura svizzero-italiana degli ultimi quarant'anni', in the
   volume *Lingua e letteratura italiana in Svizzera*, ed. by Antonio Stäuble (Bellinzona:
   Edizioni Casagrande, 1989), pp. 153–157.

Our fourth woman writer of special note, Elda Guidinetti, was born in Chiasso in 1941. Like a number of other Swiss-Italian artistic figures, she has spent time away from her native Switzerland, having lived for several years in the United States, but she now resides at Meride in the Canton Ticino. Much of her activity in recent years has been in the world of film; she was, for example, involved in the artistic direction of one of the presentations at the 1996 Locarno Film Festival. Her literary reputation rests essentially with her volume of ten short stories, *Il cortile interno esterno*.[30] It was for this volume that she was marked out by Mariangela Buogo as one of the (by now) relatively younger Swiss-Italian women writers worthy of special attention.[31] *Il cortile interno esterno* is also the title of the opening story of the collection, and furthermore it is the place where cats make love. It is also 'the condition in which the protagonists of the other stories – women, lovers, couples, men, a suicide, a mongoloid, a dog – find themselves [...] the whole expressed in an everyday literary language which is also an "external interior"'.[32]

As Antonio Stäuble puts it, the situation in which every Swiss-Italian finds him/herself is that of

the dialectic (and sometimes the tension) of belonging to Switzerland on the one hand and to Italian culture and civilisation on the other. [...] To belong to one country politically and speak the language of another, much bigger one, is not restricted to Swiss-Italians but applies to all Swiss citizens (except the Romansch-speaking ones); but for Italian-speaking Swiss this situation is stressed

---

29 Mariangela Buogo, capitolo 1, 'Svizzera Italiana: Canton Ticino: l'inquieta identità', in the Roman journal *Il Veltro*, 39, 5–6 (settembre–dicembre 1995) pp. 169–201 (p. 185). The chapter forms part of an extended overview entitled *L' 'aura italiana': culture e letterature d'oltrefrontiera, frontiera e minoranze*.

30 Elda Guidinetti, *Il cortile interno esterno* (Bellinzona: Edizioni Casagrande, 'Versanti', 1988).

31 Mariangela Buogo in *Il Veltro*, art. cit., p. 185. The other Swiss-Italian women writers mentioned are: Solvejg Albeverio Manzoni (a painter who produced a novel *Il pensatore con il mantello come meteora*, and subsequently a second novel, *Frange di solitudine*, published by Edizioni del Leone, Venice); Carla Ragni (author of *Lettera all'amore* and *La settima guglia*, published by Edizioni Il gatto dell'Ulivo), and Maria Luisa Pedotti-Pilar.

32 Dust-jacket notes to Elda Guidinetti, *Il cortile interno esterno*, op. cit.

by their extremely minoritarian and marginal position. [...] In the Ticino there are no big towns, [...] there are no publishers of international standing and the newspapers (even if proportionally quite numerous) are only read locally. These are rather prosaic facts, but they have to be borne in mind when talking of Italian Switzerland. The cultural symbiosis with Italy is much stronger than that of the other parts of Switzerland with the countries speaking their respective languages. [...] Are we then to include Italian-Swiss literature among other voices from the Italian periphery like the Sicily of Verga, Pirandello and Lampedusa, like Svevo's Trieste and the Liguria of Sbarbaro and Montale? I should say no. The Swiss component in Italian-Swiss literature is much stronger than the regional one in the aforementioned authors. That this is so is made evident by the language [...], as well as by the geographical environment described and the choice of themes. Italian Switzerland with its countryside, people, language and culture is present in most of the works of its writers.[33]

The same can clearly be said of the women writers of Italian-speaking Switzerland.[34] There has been no significant 'pull' factor simply because the writers in question are women rather than men. As Esther Spinner noted, the status of women writers 'is not a matter of extremist egalitarianism, nor of the rejection of men'.[35] No: the 'situation in Italian Switzerland is quite different. [...] A sense of grandeur and strength can only be obtained by reference to the great maternal culture of Italy. The self-confidence of this people, concentrated into the hundred kilometres between Airolo and Chiasso, is not drawn from the dialect it speaks as such, but from the language of Dante and the 50 million Italians of modern Italy'.[36] Yet there is a clear sense that 'in the literature of Italian-speaking Switzerland there are the beginnings of a new era',[37]

---

33 Antonio Stäuble, 'Italian-Swiss Literature since the Second World War', in *Modern Swiss Litertaure. Unity and Diversity*, op. cit., pp. 81–84.

34 For a chronological listing of the principal post-World War II Swiss-Italian narrative works by both men and women writers, see Andrew Wilkin, 'La narrativa svizzero-italiana dal 1945 al 1992: saggio bibliografico', in *Bulletin of the Society for Italian Studies*, number 27 (1994), pp. 21–23.

35 Esther Spinner, *Netzwerk*, 1991. This declaration is routinely quoted on printed documents by the organisation Donne che scrivono/Netzwerk schreibender Frauen/Réseau de femmes écrivains.

36 Guido Calgari, 'Italian Switzerland and National Literature', in *Swiss Men of Letters*, ed. by Alex Natan (London: Oswald Wolff, 1970), pp. 82–83.

37 Adriano Soldini, *Lettere della Svizzera Italiana. Oggi*, pamphlet, p. 5 (Zürich: Pro Helvetia, Servizio d'informazione, 1971).

and that it has indeed witnessed a marked 'literary renewal',[38] in which women writers have played a significant role. It is equally the case, however, that hard-headed realism will still be needed when discussing the position of Swiss-Italian writers, be they men or women, and the audience for which they write. A neatly pointed summary and conclusion runs as follows:

> For whom does one write? One may write for children, or one may write kitchen recipes, novels, poems, addresses for the centenaries of banks, commemorative notes for disappearing train services, school-books, volumes of memoirs, books of criticism, screenplays, or the scripts for popular radio or TV programmes. Depending on the *genre* chosen, there then follow all the usual hand-outs and 'penalties'. Then there is the question of the social status of the writer in Italian-speaking Switzerland. Professional? Teacher? Amateur? 'Sunday writer'? Someone who has been thrown out of a political party? A member of the Rotary Club? And what about relationships with publishers? Which publishers? Home publishers or foreign publishers? South of Ponte Chiasso or north of the Alps? What about consulting editors (the publisher's spies)? The critics? The non-critics? Book launches and press conferences? Reviews? Book distribution? What does it all cost? Are there any patrons or literary prizes to be had? What about cultural politics? Is the State involved? Are we thinking of Bern, Bellinzona, or Lugano? Is Pro Helvetia involved? The banks? Literary journals? And what about readers? Who reads?[39]

38 For a discussion of the elements of the post-war literary renewal in Italian-speaking Switzerland, see Andrew Wilkin, 'In margine al rinnovamento della narrativa svizzero-italiana dal 1945 ad oggi', in *Gli spazi della diversità*, op. cit.
39 This series of rhetorical questions is freely adapted from Giovanni Orelli, 'Letteratura nella Svizzera Italiana, oggi. La narrativa', in *Per conoscere la Svizzera Italiana*, op. cit., p. 106.

LIZ LOCHHEAD, ANNE CUNEO,
AMÉLIE PLUME, ISOLDE SCHAAD

Writing as a Woman in a Small Country

Round-table Discussion

An evening session of the conference was devoted to a discussion between the four writers in which members of the audience also participated. The following is an edited transcript of the proceedings.

MALCOLM PENDER: It seemed to us that the creative writers who have been publishing during the period 1971–1996 should be heard at our conference, because after all, creative writing is an important response to the kind of society in which we all live. It then occurred to us that there might well be similarities, some similarities at any rate, between Switzerland and Scotland, not in the political sense because I think the political structures are very different, but possibly in a cultural sense. For you have four literatures being written in the shadow of much larger cultures: German-Swiss literature, French-Swiss literature and Italian-Swiss literature are written in the shadow of three great European cultures, and here there is some similarity to Scotland, which is also small and where literature is also published in the shadow of a larger culture, that of England. We thought it was worth exploring these possible similarities by asking three writers from Switzerland and one from Scotland to discuss, as women writing in their respective cultures, their experience of the various pressures and influences on them. We are very pleased that they have all agreed to come along.

Firstly, there is Amélie Plume who lives in Geneva and writes in French. Her work has been appearing since the early 1980s, so that she started publishing when the suffrage which Swiss women were granted at Federal level in 1971 had been in existence for a decade, and that might or might not have had some kind of effect on her writing. She has published several novels and the last one, which I have not yet read, but whose title I think I understand very well, *Hélas nos chéris sont nos ennemis*, was published in 1995.

Anne Cuneo has a background which is indicative of the linguistic mixture which I associate with Switzerland and which I don't, I have to say, associate with Scotland. She was born in Paris and then raised partly in Italy and partly in French-speaking Switzerland and she now lives in Zürich and writes in French. Her latest novel, *Le trajet d'une rivière* published last year, has been translated into German and has been very well received. She has been publishing for longer than Amélie Plume, since just before the official emancipation of women, so possibly she will tell us of different pressures.

Isolde Schaad lives in Zürich and writes in German. She comes from a background of cultural journalism. She was for a while on the *Weltwoche*, the major Zürich weekly, and she has published several collections of essays on aspects of affluent Swiss life and once again, a title attracts me, that of her last publication *Body und Sofa. Liebesgeschichten aus der Kaufkraftklasse*.

Finally, there is Liz Lochhead whom I think most of us know. Certainly, her poetry, her work in the theatre and in television has created a very solid reputation for her. I was interested to see that she was born in Motherwell, so that probably also makes her something of a foreigner in Glasgow. I have pleasure in asking Liz Lochhead to chair the discussion.

LIZ LOCHHEAD: It's a great privilege to have been invited to come along and meet three writers, three new friends, because writers, I think, always have a great fellow-feeling for each other regardless of difficulties of language. Despite my profound ignorance of Switzerland, which is shocking and quite shameful, I very much enjoyed listening this afternoon and it was a great frustration to me that I couldn't go out and buy in translation the books that I heard being discussed. Our very profound provincialism is a great shame in this country, and I don't just mean in Scotland, I mean in Britain. One can't keep up with the works written in the English language so one doesn't work hard enough at keeping up with works in translation. And indeed, most of the books that were talked about today are apparently not even translated. It was also a surprise to me that there had only been twenty-five years of enfranchisement in Switzerland because I don't think enfranchisement and emancipation are exactly the same thing. I hope that you've had a lot longer than twenty-five years of fight towards emancipation. Emancipation is a continuing process, whereas the date of the general enfranchisement is, I think, just fact, a simple fact and only part of that process. I'm going to start off with something incomprehensible which only lasts a short time and gradually explains itself. So you're not to panic when you don't understand a word of the beginning of what I'm going to say. It is a bilingual children's poem called *Kidspoem/Bairnsang* which I was asked to write by the BBC. It ended up with a credo – something that I'd always wanted to say.

Kidspoem/Bairnsang

It wis January
and a gey dreich day
the first day I went to the school
so
ma Mum happed me up in ma good navyblue nap coat
wi the rid tartan hood
birled a scarf aroon ma neck
pu'ed on ma pixie and ma pawkies
it wis that bitter
said
'noo ye'll no starve'
gied me a wee kiss and a kidoan skelp on the bum
and sent me off across the playground
to the place I'd learn to say
It was January
and a really dismal day
the first day I went to school
so
my Mother wrapped me up in my best navyblue top coat
with the red tartan hood
twirled a scarf around my neck
pulled on my bobble-hat and mittens
it was so bitterly cold
said
'now you won't freeze to death'
gave me a little kiss and a pretend slap on the bottom
and sent me off across the playground
to the place I'd learn to forget to say
It wis January

and a gey dreich day
the first day I went to school
so
ma Mum happed me up in ma good navyblue nap coat
wi the rid tartan hood
birled a scarf aroon ma neck
pu'ed on ma pixie and ma pawkies
it was that bitter.
Oh,
saying it was one thing
but when it came to writing it
in black and white
the way it had to be said
was as if
you were grown up, posh, male, English and dead.[1]

For me the process of becoming a writer has been to stop pretending to be all these things, or at least to stop pretending to be all these things all the time, before I even lift up the pen, to write sometimes as if I'm none of these things, because I think that as a writer one wants to do everything and write in all kinds of voices. I've sometimes been on panels talking about writing as a Scot. I've rarely been asked to talk about writing as a Scottish woman. So as well as writing as a woman in Scotland, I'm also writing as a woman in a small country and also writing as a woman in a large country if I count the whole of the British Isles as my country, which at times I do, although I strongly identify with this wee one. Sometimes I write as a writer in a large country, with an even larger potential market or readership in the huge English-speaking world. So I think these identities don't exclude each other, one is all of these things at different times.

The four of us are going each to make a little statement and then we're going to throw it open for discussion and questions. At the end, each of the Swiss writers is going to read a little bit in her own language, because even although some of us don't understand, it is a privilege and a pleasure to hear writers reading their own words in their own rhythms. Listening this afternoon, I was fascinated by how many words come up again and again in my own consciousness. I was very moved

1 *Penguin Modern Poets Volume 4*: Liz Lochhead, Roger McGough, Sharon Olds (London: Penguin, 1995), pp. 61–2

and delighted when Amélie Plume said 'Well, of course we don't talk about these things. We're writers, you know, it's not our job to come up with overviews or academic ideas of why we do our work.' Quite often critics explain to us all why we've done things. It's not that what they are saying is not true or correct but it's just that's not why we've done it, or that way round. We haven't had the thesis first and then written something to explore that thesis. In fact, certain writing sometimes goes dead because one feels that the writer has done that, has had the theory. I'm thinking of a poet I like very much, Adrienne Rich, and before she became such a theorist I enjoyed her poetry more. So in a way, as writers it's our job to dramatise and explore these issues without having a kind of theoretical or academic overview of them. Of course, as we write we become more conscious of what we think and feel, and what we think and feel gets closer together as we make the writing more conscious and more alive. I just wanted to end up my little speech with a list of words that came up again and again this afternoon, words that have come up either when I've been talking about writing but even have come up in the shadowy world journey of things that one wants to write about. They are words like *identity, role model, mother-figure, mother-tongue, shadowy world, journey, unknown, secret, monsters, grotesque, history, reclamation, myth, survival, mixture of high language and dialect.* I'd now like to invite Isolde to start off by talking to us about her personal experience of being a woman writer in a small country.

ISOLDE SCHAAD: Thank you. Of course, I'm not as gifted as my host in the Scottish language or shall I say English or British or International. I would love to say International, obviously that's not the case for me. I can't say sometimes I'm writing for a large country. That's the only thing I'm not in a position to say. We have a really limited audience in German-speaking Switzerland, yet we belong to a world-language — German. I think I'm not really like the English or Spanish people who covered a whole world so usually if somebody asks me 'What is your profession?' and if I say 'I'm a writer', there is normally the following reaction: 'Oh, you are a writer! How very interesting! But what do you actually do?' It is a casual remark but it depicts the image of a writer in a German-speaking culture. A writer, especially a single female, is a kind of intellectual involved in an obscure activity. And there is still a fear, I think, of an intellectual single woman in German culture or German-speaking culture, particularly in small countries. It is not like in France or in the United States where the single intellectual woman has a higher reputation. It has been hard work and still is hard work for them. But writing as a woman in a small country means, as we have heard several times in the case of Switzerland, to be part of a very small minority, firstly as a member of one of four national languages, secondly as a woman writer and this specific situation creates both advantages and contradictions. In the German-speaking part of Switzerland, we tend to be orientated towards our northern neighbour, to mighty Germany which plays the leading role in German-language publishing. Although we are professionally and mentally in a small province of Germany, socially we lead an urban life in Switzerland, that's a contradiction. Living in such a small region we are not anonymous as women writers and often we are more recognised for our political standpoint, for our social outlook, for our left-wing voting or right-wing voting than for our writing. I think we are more public figures, asked to participate in all sorts of campaigns, but not actually for our writing, and people say 'I'm sorry, I haven't read your latest book. I'm sorry, I would like to read it but I haven't read it. But of course, you are a name for me.' That's a very big contradiction which I have experienced for a long time. Of course we would prefer to be read rather than be heard. The other thing is, we women have no lobby like our male colleagues in Switzerland who have a particular thing that we might call a *Stammtisch*. Perhaps a *Stammtisch* is something like an English club, only less formal. But it is still a kind of organisation: men have more links to one another through organisations, they really relate to one another.

I want to reserve the word 'network' for my sex. We have started to found a kind of network of writing women in Switzerland and I think that is good although it causes a new problem, that of being organised, which also has advantages and contradictions. There is another problem which we are facing, although I must say we are quite privileged in Switzerland as Beatrice von Matt beautifully outlined this afternoon. We have really rich, intense writing in Switzerland compared with the smallness of the country, and this has been going on for the last twenty years. But now we are confronted with a new influx of international conquerors created by the book market. I would not like to use the word Americanisation although all the booksellers are using it. Domestic writing is rather pushed back in favour of the international market for best-selling books in translation. So sometimes we are in the position where we have literary talk-shows on Swiss television in which German critics invite German guests or perhaps an American guest even a German-speaking guest in order to talk about the latest German novel or the latest American translation, whereas we Swiss writing in German are actually excluded from this kind of showcase which is there only to promote internationalised production in the book market.

AMÉLIE PLUME : Thank you very much for having invited me. When I was invited I said I cannot speak in English and Joy said, 'Not important. Everybody will help you.' So I hope you will. I start by saying that I came from the Canton in Switzerland which first gave the vote to women in 1959 so when I was eighteen years old I received a cantonal vote as something quite normal. It was a very good experience. I have written a short text with five points to present 'Writing as a Woman in Switzerland'.

1. In Switzerland, years ago :

GIRL :   Mother, I would like to become a writer.
MOTHER :   What an idea, darling!
GIRL :   I like writing, Mam.
MOTHER :   You can write for your pleasure, but it's not a job.
GIRL :   There are a lot of writers around the world.
MOTHER :   Not in Switzerland, darling.
GIRL :   And Ramuz?
MOTHER :   He is the exception that confirms the rule.
GIRL :   Is that true, Mam?
MOTHER :   In Switzerland writers are French, darling, and good writers dead. Anyway they are all men. It is nothing for you.
GIRL :   What about George Sand and Colette, Mam?
MOTHER :   They are also dead and anyway their lives are not specially a good example to follow.
GIRL :   Why, Mam?
MOTHER :   You will understand later and now can you stop talking, please, and help me to wash the dishes.
GIRL :   Yes Mam.

2. Abroad, later on :

Where do you come from?
From Switzerland.

Oh! It's a beautiful country!
Yes.
..And rich!
Yes.
You have big mountains!
Yes.
And cows!
Yes.
And chocolate!
Yes.
And watches!
Yes.
And banks!
Yes.
And ...
And writers.
Oh, you have writers in Switzerland? I didn't know that.
Yes, we have writers.
What do they write?
Novels, short stories, poetry, anything.
I've never heard about that. Do they all write in Swiss?
Swiss does not exist.
It's strange, I have a feeling to have heard about a very special old language spoken in Switzerland.
Yes it does exists. It is called Romansch and it is one of our four national languages.
Four national languages in such a small country!
Yes, French, German, Italian and Romansch.
You have writers writing in those four different languages?
Yes.
Isn't it crazy?
Oh yes, it's crazy.

3. In Switzerland, 1996:

I became a writer. I wrote and published seven books. They are sold in bookstores, I have readers, some reviews in newspapers and on the radio.

4. Abroad, 1996:

I have been invited with two other Swiss women writers to the University of Strathclyde to speak about Writing as a Woman in Switzerland.

5. Conclusion:

Does not that story seem to show that miracles happen not only in grottos with poor shepherdesses, doesn't it?

ANNE CUNEO: It won't look like it at the beginning, but I'm not straying from the subject. I was born in Paris of Italian parents. I was raised in northern Italy and in Lausanne, Switzerland and also in Plymouth, England. My being Swiss is a sheer accident, I'm only Swiss because I married a Swiss man, or rather, a Swiss man married me. In fact, I've also been an Italian all my life. Italians can keep their nationality, I've kept it and I must admit to everybody tonight that as such, I've always had the vote. I cannot remember any day of my conscious life when I couldn't have gone and voted, only I've been voting for a country and for politicians of a country I wasn't living in, but I've had the vote all my life. When I became Swiss and realised that I didn't have the vote at federal level – I had it at cantonal level because I was in a canton which already had it – I found it ridiculous. But my position being what it was, it never really preoccupied me. So I am Swiss by accident. That was the first point. Secondly, I was born in Paris with a twin brother who died days after our birth. We were very rare things from the same egg. My being the girl is complete accident. This accident is significant on the political level since I have been discriminated against like every woman here but also I'm sure like every Scottish woman and man within Great Britain, like every Jew within the Gentile environment and like every black person in a white environment. But personally, I refuse to see myself as a woman who writes in a small country. I write, fullstop. This is the only fact which I am ready to accept and the place where I write ignores categories. In the space where writing takes place there are no women and no men, no blacks and no whites, no young and no old, no Swiss, no French, no English. There aren't even literary and non-literary texts, writers or non-writers in other words. So one might discuss the subsequent distribution of our writing, its reception, but I, for one, have nothing to say on the subject of writing as a woman in a small country. I write as a human being in a large world. I have never written books for a particular public, I have never in fact written for anyone but myself. This was of course not deliberate, but looking back, I think it was the right thing to do, most probably the only thing to do. I also think that in the long run, it is not helping women to speak of women's writing. It is not helping blacks to speak of Negro literature, or Jews to speak of Jewish literature. That only maintains ghettos which are a bit more subtle than political, racist ghettos but which are just as unmistakably and fatally there. As for myself, I have spoken in my books of my experiences as a human being including, once or twice, of my experiences as a woman, but I cannot help noticing that my greatest success to date is a book in which I, an Italian woman whom circumstances have made a Swiss writer, have written the autobiography of a man who was an Englishman and who lived in the 16th century and who, on top of everything, was a musician whereas I don't know anything about music. Once again, I didn't do this on purpose and when the book was finished and no-one had read it, my brain was obsessed with the fact that, as a woman, I shouldn't have dared. I thought this book which I took years to write and which was so much work, was going to be my greatest flop. I really thought this until the first reactions came. I'm very happy that it turned out to be, in fact, even on a modest scale, my greatest success. It gave more impetus still to my idea that the only way one can create, in whichever field, is by daring to look beyond one's condition of black, of Jew, of old, of young, of woman, of man and in order to be just a human being, which is a tall enough order.

LIZ LOCHHEAD: It now seems a good time to throw the discussion open.

IRENE MACKINTOSH: I just wanted to ask a question about dialect and spoken language. I know that in literature there is a huge discrepancy between dialect, what people actually speak and what people write, which was exemplified perfectly in your poem and I wondered if that came up in Swiss literature. To what extent are you affected by the fact that you're writing something you don't say?

ANNE CUNEO: Every written language is another form of its spoken language. With German-Swiss, they are two different languages. But I'd say I don't write the same French as I speak. You don't write the same English as you speak.

ISOLDE SCHAAD: This is a really big question. We have every now and then movements which try to renew dialect, *Mundart* writing, and we have quite a lot of poetry in dialect. On the other hand we are of course more orientated towards the German culture in German-speaking Switzerland

and it means that we really think differently when we are writing. All the time you are writing you are thinking in German, of course it might be a peculiar kind of German and we have a kind of high German-Swiss. Even Max Frisch and Dürrenmatt are representative of a kind of high German-Swiss which has been cultivated. At first it was regarded as a disadvantage in publishing and we remember when the prestigious German publisher Suhrkamp always corrected colloquial terms like *Trottoir*, for instance, for we have a lot of French words in German Swiss, and there was the German word *Gehsteig*, and we thought this was very strange. Nowadays it might even be an advantage to have a kind of a colloquial vocabulary and Suhrkamp Verlag does not correct it any longer. On the contrary, it's almost the opposite. The Austrians also have a particular problem. They have a kind of idiom, and in their writing this is regarded more as evidence of the richness of the German languages, since we have to distinguish different kinds of German. But if I'm writing, during the process of writing I'm actually thinking in German, which is different.

FAUSTO FERRARI: On the Italian side, Ticino still has Ticinese dialect but in Italy we used to talk Lombard. For example I can talk dialect which is understood in Lugano and Milan but they don't speak it in Milan any more. I'm from Italian-speaking Switzerland so, funnily enough, in Swiss-Italian they're keeping to the dialect but only just. The Italians have lost it altogether.

ISOLDE SCHAAD: I must admit, for myself, I do not approve of forcing dialect writing. I'm rather internationally minded. Dialect can have, as Frau Simmen mentioned, an emotional aspect. It can be a special medium but for literary writing I think we have a rich language, German, and we can use it.

ALLYSON FIDDLER: My question is a comment and it is away from the dialect issue. It is to Anne Cuneo. I found it very interesting, this space where you write. You said there is no distinction between the sexes and between classes and races, but writers are of course of necessity, also readers. I'm wondering about this space where we read and whether that can ever be free from distinctions, whether when we read we must necessarily read as a woman, as a white middle-class British woman.

ANNE CUNEO: Well, I don't know. I'm sure we read because we have had an education and so on. This being said, I don't know how you read. I go into bookshops or into the public library and I just take any books, and I don't look at who has written it in which language, I just look to see if there is something that catches my eye. I read it and whether the writer is a woman or a man, a German or an Englishman or whatever, just does not matter to me at all. You cannot write except from the unconscious and the unconscious has no colour. There is a part in the unconscious which is called woman and man but there is also a part where you are both woman and man, where you are both black and white, where you are both oppressed and oppressor, because your unconscious takes up much more than what you are.

LIZ LOCHHEAD: I agree that the absolute aim of writing is a kind of androgyny, but I don't think it is easy to achieve that and I definitely don't think that one can achieve that as a reader, not automatically. It is not about who wrote it, it's about who you are reading it. You cannot deny your own experience.

ANNE CUNEO: Well, I'm not making any theory about reading. I just say I never look at who the writer is, and I've never read a woman because she was a woman, or a man because he was a man apart from when I'm working as a journalist and I have to know the point of view of a South African.

ISOLDE SCHAAD: I think really language is a barrier. We can see it from translation. Sometimes you don't recognise your own text in a different language. I think this is a different way of thinking and we think differently in English than we think in French or in Siberian or in whatever. I think we are culturally formed by our language and education but of course there is a kind of Utopian feeling I share with Anne. I wish it was like what I experience, but it is not. That's a contradiction we maybe have and I understand what she means, and of course you are very talented. You have command of almost five languages, you read perfectly, that's a real privilege and we are more limited. What I do not like about this dialect fashion is the diminutive. We have a Swiss language which is *Schweizli* which always puts an 'i' at the end. It diminishes our own consciousness and this is really what I do not like about this dialect writing. It is so neat and it is so *herzig* and it is just what we need to abolish. That's why I really have to make a difference. I'm a great admirer and was a friend of Niklaus Meienberg and he invented a new prose which is a mixture, something else altogether.

COMMENT FROM THE FLOOR: When you look back to Gotthelf, there is an immense richness of dialect there which we have lost because we were looking towards Germany. In many dialects there are a lot of verbs, for example, when you look at the Bernese dialect there is an immense amount of verbs for all sorts of things which over 20, 30, 40 years have been gradually lost. This must be true of many other dialects in Switzerland as well. A lot has been lost because we have been looking towards Germany and now there has been a sort of a rediscovering. This is a hypothesis, I don't really know, I haven't been living in Switzerland for many years. What do you think?

ANNE CUNEO: I'm looking at this a bit from the outside, but in my opinion, someone like Robert Walser or Friedrich Glauser used dialect extensively in their German extensively, but in a very subtle way not in a programmatic way like Meienberg did, but it never really got lost. Or in this book by Jürg Steiner, *Das Netz zerreisen,* which takes place in a café in Biel on the border between French-speaking and German-speaking Switzerland. But the novel is all in German, and it is all in the café and he refers all the time to what people say. There is no dialogue in dialect, but I thought there was a strong Swiss-German influence on the German. I love those books and I love those writers.

COMMENT FROM THE FLOOR: I am German and Swiss and was raised for the first ten years of my life in Germany and I think we Swiss overestimate this gap between High German and spoken German because it is the same gap in Germany as well. A Bavarian doesn't speak what he writes. I remember because I had one of those wonderful colourful Cologne accents and I was told at school 'You should speak proper German in Germany!' The same gap exists everywhere in the German-speaking parts of the world.

REGINA WECKER: It's considered proper to speak dialect in Switzerland and when I grew up in Berlin, it was not considered proper to speak the Berlin dialect. That's the difference. It just depends on whether you decide that this is an audience where you address the audience in High German, then it's not proper to speak dialect. But with your parents you speak dialect. My mother always told me not to speak the Berlin dialect with her.

UTE PENDER: My question is about this networking. I wondered who is networked. Is it Swiss writers who are networking? French-speaking, German-speaking, Italian-speaking woman writers? What is the purpose of the networking? To get each other translated into the various languages?

ISOLDE SCHAAD: To get more interchange of information, for example. There is also the matter of the publishers. I myself have rather an ambiguous view on that but I still think it is important to be a member of the women's movement, although we would hope that some day we will not need it any more. But the problem arises where publishers and the top rank television people are men. But still it is worthwhile to exchange views, to give help, for instance, to arrange readings for young authors. We recently arranged readings for young unknown women writers.

AMÉLIE PLUME: There are translation subsidies within the Confederation between the languages but it comes maybe five to eight years after the original publication, so I belong to an association with other writers, for example with Isolde. But I don't know what she writes, I don't read in German and it's a little bit strange to have friends from your country and you don't know what they write.

ROSEMARIE SIMMEN: As has been said, the Confederation gives subsidies for translating. We also try in the Swiss Arts Council either to give subsidies for translating books, or to give subsidies to translators for them to translate what they think is worthwhile. So we don't choose the books but give the money, just as we give the money to writers, for instance 7,000 francs, which should allow you to write for a certain period, to stop other work and to be able to write. For the last three or four years, we have been doing this also for translators and I hope to avoid the consequence that we were talking about, namely, that it is always so late. We give it directly to people who know better than the cultural bureaucrats. But I don't know whether you have any experience with this. Does it really work or is it too short a period to know if it does?

ANNE CUNEO: German-speaking writers actually have no barrier to going to Germany. If the publisher has a good distribution they can sell books in Germany. But French-speaking publishers simply have no existence on the other side of the border. They have all tried and they have all failed or almost failed. It only works when a Swiss publisher associates himself with a French publisher and then you get French distribution. Or when we ourselves manage to be published by a Paris publisher. But it is the cultural imperialism of France which causes that.

ISOLDE SCHAAD: Of course, only the very prominent Swiss writers are published by the great German houses and I'm not even sure if this is preferable for the Swiss. For example, in my situation, I went to a Swiss publisher on purpose, since the first book I published was on a particularly Swiss issue so I thought that perhaps the audience would really be in Switzerland. But of course, we also have the problem of the prophet in his own country who is only recognised if he is successful abroad. If he has good reviews in German papers then the Swiss will ask for him. And that is a problem of imperialism. It is a kind of imperialism created by great countries in Europe like France and Germany.

ANNE CUNEO: There is, of course, this paradox that French-speaking storytelling is very, very strong and well-developed. The number of good storytellers in France in, say, the last forty years is just amazing. There are just as many amazing storytellers in Montpellier or Marseilles as in Paris. But in Paris it's the system that revolves in an enclosed way, and you have these people who write, not for themselves, but who write thinking of the critics, thinking of the reception before they write. And this kills them. If you take for the last ten years the awards of the *Prix Goncourt* which is supposed to be the best French book of the year, there is not one that really carries you. There are so many provincial writers and this is a whole problem in itself from which Canadians, Belgians and Swiss suffer most. For we are not unique in that. You have now and then a Belgian writer who succeeds in Paris or a Canadian who succeeds in Paris and Paris has a way of just absorbing him, of saying 'Look, we are very good with Canada' and that's it. There are another fifty coming behind if they can wait a generation.

LIZ LOCHHEAD: I think we could transpose that into London quite well. So it's not a matter of French, it's a matter of Paris? It's not a matter of the English, it's a matter of London. It's the big imperial capital.

ANDREW WILKIN: Two points, if I may. There is a degree of divergence here because I wouldn't want those in the audience to go away thinking that we're simply discussing the problems of imperialistic Germany or France. I would like to establish the Italian circumstances for you, which are entirely different. Two very good friends of mine, Giovanni Orelli and Grytzko Mascioni are published in Italy, highly successfully. And two women, Alice Ceresa and Fleur Jaeggy, both publish in Italy in very successful major publishing houses which seems to indicate that things are different in the cultural context of the Italophone world. Ticinese and Grigionese are not rejected, if that's the appropriate word, as perhaps French-Swiss and German-Swiss are. I'd also like to second what Frau Simmen said, because the one dimension that needs to come across really rather strongly is that Switzerland has said to itself: Switzerland has a culture, and it is to the credit of Pro Helvetia, the Swiss Arts Council, that this has happened. The fact that this culture has constituent elements which are expressed in French, German, Italian and Romansch, is another matter. Pro Helvetia has facilitated the opportunity for Swiss works of whichever of the four national languages to be translated into the other three national languages and this means that a Swiss in the north of the country need not be ignorant of the culture of the Swiss of the south of the country or east or west or vice versa and this is something which is to be highly commended.

ISOLDE SCHAAD: You are right but this is still the theory and not the practice. We are on the way but it takes a long time. As Amélie has said, we can ask for it, but it can take seven or eight years till our book is even on the list for recommendation to be published in French and that happens to us.

MALCOLM PENDER: Could I come back to a point that Isolde made which raises this whole question of ambivalence to the large neighbour. You talked about the Swiss buying a book if it is published in a German publishing house. I'd always thought that a German-Swiss writer would go to a German publishing house so that he could get into the German publishing market. But, in fact, the thing that startled me in an article that I was reading recently, was that four-fifths of the sales of the average German-Swiss novel published by a German publishing house are in Switzerland, so it's the *imprimatur* of German culture which causes the Swiss to buy the German-Swiss book.

LIZ LOCHHEAD: But this always happens, doesn't it, in countries that are in the shadow of a dominant culture. I think it happens in Scotland a lot. I think it happens in film, I remember when Bill Forsyth made *Gregory's Girl*. When it was a success in London and America, then the Scots really wanted to come and see it in the cinema. Before that it had been a wee Scottish film. I think we internalise these questions of inferiority but it's definitely nice for everybody to feel validated by the larger society. What is wonderful is when self-confidence arises when people can feel the right to say it's a small country without having to get on the London train or the Paris train or the Berlin train to sign a contract. Small countries, but they are not that small if one is talking to those countries, one is still talking the truth to quite a large audience, I think. I know that working in the theatre, it doesn't really bother me if nobody does it in London so long as I can keep working. I don't feel as if I live in a provincial city in Britain. I feel as if I live in the capital of another country, and I know that's not even true. That's another thing I wanted to ask. Friends of mine have talked about the position of Scotland with regard to the dominant culture. You were allowed to be a Scottish writer, you weren't allowed to be a Scottish woman writer, because the Scot was already 'the other' in terms of the dominant culture. To be Scottish, to be Celtic, was 'the other' anyway and if you were another 'other', a woman, that was just too much. So that I've found, certainly in the past and I don't know if this is changing, that here in Britain there was definitely a taste for a certain kind of Scottish writing, but it tended to be for male, machismo and often Glaswegian writing. You weren't allowed to write as a middle-class woman writer, Glaswegian or Aberdonian or anything else. There was a certain kind of Scottishness that was desired by 'the other' which was to be very, very masculine, so there was a sort of male machismo Glaswegian Scottish school of writing that was accepted all over Britain. There is still a Glaswegian cultural imperialism. I've heard this expressed by Highland writers I know or rural writers I know, I think even by Edinburgh writers until Irvine Welsh knocked everybody for six by having a best-seller all over Britain. You're allowed to be a Scot, but only a certain kind of Scot. Are you allowed to be Swiss, but only a certain kind of Swiss? Do you have this experience?

ISOLDE SCHAAD: We have regional springs in literature. Now it's the Austrian spring, now it's the Swiss spring. We have a blossoming of literature and everybody wants to have this kind of writing, but fortunately it only lasts for two or three seasons, then the next spring comes. It is also a matter of the market as I was saying. There is much more pressure on bookselling nowadays than previously, and much less is actually being sold. I doubt if it is only television, but the booksellers in Zürich claim that they are selling less than ten years ago and that the number of readers is decreasing. On the other hand, a peculiar thing is that 90% of the readers are women and women readers are the ones who go to the readings given by writers.

LIZ LOCHHEAD: I wanted to ask something that came up slightly earlier today. I know that it was by a complete chance it was German-Swiss literature that was talked about this afternoon because no one had consulted before. Is that the kind of chance that would always happen? Does that reflect an actual imbalance within the country of Switzerland?

ANNE CUNEO: Frau Simmen will not contradict me when I say: if you don't take great care of your minorities, they will become forgotten, because 75% of Swiss speak German or 70% and 25% French and they are already a minority, and 5% speak Italian, and then there is a very, very small minority, I don't know if it is 1% which speaks Romansch, but they tend to get forgotten.

ISOLDE SCHAAD: You are right, that is usually the case, but there is also a phenomenon which I call the 'Ethnobonus'. That means that we are now at a point when regionalism is really being fostered, which might have both positive and negative aspects. We have a kind of movement towards poetry and we have a lot of really exotic writing being translated. These trends are now highly appreciated even though the critics don't know the language. I think it's a very good thing to have Romansch but I think every one of the ten Romansch writers now has an advantage in comparison with the very large number of German writers, for example. There are two sides to the point.

ANNE CUNEO: A little advantage and then the great disadvantage of minorities, and I'm not now speaking of the French minorities because we still have France. We are not such a minority, but for the real minorities, the great difficulty is that there is one season for them and then they get forgotten for ten years and then again, one season and they have this bonus but the bonus comes and goes all the time, so I would say the minus cancels out the bonus.

UTE PENDER: When Isolde says there is imbalance, that in Romansch everyone gets published, I remember that when I asked 'Is it difficult to get published?', one writer claimed: 'Well, it's actually difficult *not* to get published.' But the point of my question really is: are there any steps that are being taken to balance this out or is it just market forces which determine that so many are published in one particular language? Are there positive steps being taken so that more French writing should be published, more Romansch, more Italian?

ROSEMARIE SIMMEN: First of all, I want to say that there is a difference whether you belong to a minority that is a minority within Switzerland, or whether you belong to a minority that is an absolute minority, and for Romansch there are a few linguistic islands in Italy, but taken all together that's really a very small minority, and you are partly right when you say that you are spoilt when you are a Romansch writer, then you will be published anyway and it's much harder for the majority, for the writers in the majority but that's true to a certain extent for German-Swiss writers, it's a matter of whether it is more or less difficult, while for Romansch it is a question of to be or not to be. It will die out if they don't get any help, so if we consider that these four languages are part of our national identity, then we have to do it. There are some who say: 'Forget about it, they won't be able to survive so why do you want to keep them alive artificially?' But I don't share that point of view. As for the other languages, there are, of course, Italian and French, that's not French as a world language, only as a minority in Switzerland where conditions are different, I would say. To conclude, we always spoke about *épées*, swords, for majorities and minorities – it is not the absolute size which counts, but those for the minorities have to be a little bit longer, for eventually this makes everything the same size. Majorities have to be more careful about minorities than they would be mathematically.

LIZ LOCHHEAD: I'd like to ask each of you to read something very short in its original language.

ANNE CUNEO: I want to explain why I'm reading this. Between three and eight years ago I wrote a book about this English musician I was telling you about. He's a Cornishman and to write about a Cornishman I had to get help. So there is one specialist of Tudor Cornwall, A. L. Rowse, a great historian and a very original character. He was extremely nice and he said to me: 'Look, if you want to write about Francis Tregian who is completely uninteresting, go ahead. I never discourage anybody. But I want to make a deal with you. I'll help you, you help me.' So I said 'Yes, OK.' And then came the real surprise, he said: 'Well, in the course of my studies when I wasn't looking for it, I have found out who Shakespeare's Dark Lady was. I've written a history book about it and I've mentioned this in all kinds of history books and people don't really believe me, so I thought a good novel would do it, but I am no novelist. I'll help you write your novel and then you write my novel.' And that's what I did and I'm going to read you one page of this novel.

Of course, in writing this novel, I had to make lots of choices because Shakespeare has been interpreted in about five thousand ways. I
adopted as the Dark Lady A. L. Rowse's Dark Lady, because that was
the deal. There is a storyteller who is not Shakespeare and not the Dark
Lady, but Mr Shakespeare's apprentice:

> Nous rentrions de chez Lord Strange et étions à Tower Street. Je précédais mon
> compagnon pour lui frayer un chemin en vociférant comme je l'avais vu faire
> à Ned. Avec un rire amusé, Master Will m'avait glissé :
> 'On dirait que tu n'as jamais rien fait d'autre de ta vie.'
> 'Comme vous le soir où vous attachiez les chevaux,' ai-je murmuré entre
> deux cris.
> Il a ri de plus belle. Nous nous amusions, il faut le dire, tous les deux.
> Tower Street a soudain été mise sens dessus dessous par un cri semblable au
> mien : 'Prenez le large ! Faites place, faites place !' Sauf que ce n'était pas ma voix
> fluette d'adolescent qui le lançait, mais le chœur stentorien de quatre valets à
> cheval vêtus d'une splendide livrée bleue bordée d'argent qui précédaient une
> voiture scintillante d'or et de soieries, attelée à deux chevaux d'un blanc im
> maculé. Une vision de rêve.
> Aujourd'hui, nous sommes habitués à voir des équipages traverser à toute
> allure les rues populeuses, précédés de valets en livrée qui se frayent un passage
> en écrasant quiconque ne vide pas immédiatement les lieux. Il y a dix ans, c'était
> rare, et toute Tower Street s'est figée pour voir le spectacle.
> Lorsque le véhicule est arrivé à notre hauteur, la physionomie de Master Will
> s'est transformée. Il a pâli extrêmement, ses yeux avaient l'intense fixité de la
> passion, et sa langue passait et repassait sur ses lèvres soudain déssechées. J'ai
> suivi son regard, et j'ai reconnu Madame Emilia. Elle était vêtue aussi somp
> tueusement que la première fois, reposée sur un monceau de coussins et – il
> n'y a pas d'autre mot – se donnait à voir avec une arrogance insoutenable qui
> l'a rendue presque laide à mes yeux.
> Rien de tel pour Master Will.
> Elle l'a vu, l'a reconnu, a fait un signe de tête condescendant. Il a ôté son
> chapeau et s'est incliné sans la quitter du regard. Il est resté figé ainsi, le front
> sur l'encolure de son cheval, longtemps après qu'elle fut passée et il a fallu que
> je l'appelle plusieurs fois avant qu'il ne réagisse.
> 'Tu as vu cela ?'
> 'Oui. C'était Madame Bassano, la favorite de Lord Hunsdon.'
> 'Elle est tout simplement fascinante.'
> Je n'ai pas renchéri, et il m'a regardé, ironique.
> 'Tu désapprouves ?'
> 'Moi, monsieur ? Je n'ai pas à juger. Je trouve comme vous que cette dame
> a de très beaux yeux.'
> Il a éclaté d'un rire qui a découvert ses dents blanches et je me souviens

d'avoir pensé qu'elles scintillaient de bonheur. Il a tourné son regard du côté
où l'équipage avait disparu, et a dit à mi-voix :
'Ce printemps de l'amour me rappelle l'incertaine gloire d'une journée d'avril.
Un instant le soleil dévoile sa splendeur ; L'instant suivant, un nuage a tout effacé.'
Il a ponctué ses paroles d'une de ces grandes tapes auxquelles mes épaules
avaient fini par se faire, et nous avons poussé nos chevaux.
Quelque chose d'important s'était produit. Je l'ai senti, c'est pour cela que
cette rencontre est restée imprimée en moi dans ses moindres détails.[2]

AMÉLIE PLUME : I'm going to read a first page of my last book *Hélas
nos chéris sont nos ennemis*. It's a lot of complaints by women and I have
organised them like a symphony, during one day and it's breakfast, with
women and children and the stress :

Deux cent dix centilitres d'eau bouillie, mon Dieu déjà 7h30, refroidir, oui
au revoir Pierre bonne journée, je vais être en retard, sept mesurettes de lait
en poudre, agiter, vérifier la tétine, il faut que j'y aille, ne tire pas les pieds
du bébé Barnabé tu vas le faire pleurer, au revoir Paul bonne journée finis ta
tartine Méline et toi ton chocolat chaud Arnaud. Carsten! Carsten! tu des-
cends? tu peux t'habiller seul Laurent tu es grand maintenant, bonne journée à toi aussi Jacques, s'il te plaît Heidi ne laisse pas Didier vider le sucrier
ni Juliette le lait à côté de l'assiette, au revoir Jean bonne journée, c'est aga-
çant Carsten n'est pas descendu, Carsten! Carsten! laisse-moi t'aider Henri
tu vois bien que tu es trop petit, ta tartine Méline, ton chocolat chaud Arnaud, je vais être en retard, Didier pose ce sucrier, pas à côté de l'assiette Juliette, au revoir Pierre, au revoir Paul, au revoir Jacques, au revoir Jean, il faut
absolument que j'y aille, s'il te plaît Juliette dans l'assiette, non Didier pas le
sucrier, bonne journée, dépêchez-vous on y va, au revoir, ta tartine Méline,
ton chocolat chaud Arnaud, Carsten! Carsten! au revoir au revoir, alors ce
petit renvoi ça vient Cornélia?
Vous avez bien compris les gosses? Si un monsieur vous offre un bonbon
vous dites non merci Monsieur et s'il insiste vous répétez non non non et s'il
vous prend par la main pour vous emmener en promenade vous criez au secours au secours! – Au secours! Au secours! Comme ça fort Maman? – Oui,
comme ça fort.[3]

ISOLDE SCHAAD : I'm going to read two pieces : first, a *Leitmotiv,* I have

2 Anne Cuneo, *Objets de splendeur. M. Shakespeare amoureux* (Yvonand : Cam-
piche,1996), pp. 76–78.
3 Amélie Plume, *Hélas nos chéris sont nos ennemis* (Genève : Zoé, 1995), pp. 11–12.

learnt it is even used in English, a *Leitmotiv* from the book which contains life stories and love stories. The partner turns out not to have been a human being all along:

> 'Ich bin das DING, und das Ding ist dein Herr, und du sollst in ihm Glanz erhalten, als elender Verbraucher. Ich bin das Ding, das dich erhebt aus dem Jammerthal der Gelüste, die namenlos sind, ich bin dein Name, und du bist mein. Ich gebe dir und deinesgleichen, die im Kreatürlichen krepieren, eine Zweckbestimmung: Du bist durch mich, und ich bin in dir. Ich bin das Ding, das deinem lichtscheuen Tun, deinen schlüpfrigen, hinterhältigen und anonymen Bedürfnissen einen Sinn gibt, so dass sie nicht verkommen im Elend der Anfechtung. Dass sie nicht verkannt werden, sondern erkannt, im Tonus meines Rauschens. Im Spiegel meiner Aura sollst du dich schauen, so dass du dich hinweghebst über die miese Genügsamkeit. Im Aroma meiner Anwesenheit sollst du atmen und im Echo meiner Präsenz existieren! Erkenne mich, und du wirst dich in mir erkennen, im Lichte des Logo und Styling, so dass du durch sie Charakter erhältst und Profil. Siehe, ohne mich, das Ding, bist du nichts!' [4]

I'm now going to read a short text which refers to our main topic of 25 years emancipation. It is about male politicians' language in Switzerland. *Exclusiv-Interview*: it's a politician giving an interview:

> 'Luegedzi. Ich bin der Meinung, dass wir in dieser Frage der Ansicht sind. Und ich stehe dazu, dass ich meine, es ist an der Zeit, auf der Tagesordnung der Sache zu sein, deren Ansicht wir sind. Ich meine, dass wir alle dazu stehen, müssen und können, der Ansicht zu sein, was wir immer gesagt haben, im Sinne einer Meinung. Luegedzi, ich bin der Meinung, man muss miteinander reden, damit wir alle der Ansicht werden können, die ich hier ganz persönlich vertrete, ich betone ausdrücklich, persönlich, mein Kollege wird ihnen bestätigen, dass unsere Meinung ganz persönlich die ist, die an der Zeit ist.
>
> Wozu wir, wie ich meine, alle stehen können, in der Ansicht, die wir immer vertreten haben. Ich meine, Herr Schreiber, wir haben immer deutlich gesagt, dass die Sache *die* ist. Ich bin der Ansicht, man sollte den Tatsachen ins Auge blicken, die unsere Meinung sind, deren Ansicht wir immer waren. Herr Schreiber, lassen Sie sich das gesagt sein, wir müssen heute umdenken, daran kommt keiner vorbei, der der Ansicht ist. Es ist bekannt, dass die Meinung immer unser Boden der Grundhaltung gewesen ist, den wir haben. Als eine

4 Isolde Schaad, *Body und Sofa. Liebesgeschichten aus der Kaufkraftklasse* (Zürich: Limmat Verlag, 1994), p. 7.
5 Isolde Schaad, *Küsschen Tschüss. Sprachbilder und Geschichten zur öffentlichen Psychologie* (Zürich: Limmat Verlag, 1989), pp. 186–7.

nicht wegzudiskutierende Tatsache, die in der Natur der Sache liegt. Ich meine, dass es an der Zeit ist, der Natur der Sache, die eine Tatsache ist, auf der wir bestehen, endlich ins Auge zu blicken. In der Meinung, die wir immer vertreten haben.'[5]

MALCOLM PENDER: I'd like, on behalf of the audience, to refer to the foreigner whom Amélie Plume spoke about in her introductory remarks, that foreigner who asked, 'Do all these writers write in Swiss?' Now we know that Swiss, in fact, is extremely complicated. I think that's part of the process of learning about something, realising its complications. So we'd like to thank Amélie Plume, Anne Cuneo and Isolde Schaad for coming and telling us about these complications. I'd also like to thank Liz Lochhead who, I think, has conducted the proceedings with humour, which indeed, I would say, substantiates your claim that you've lived in Glasgow for thirty years. I'd like you all to join with me in thanking all four ladies.

Joy Charnley, Malcolm Pender, Andrew Wilkin

Interview with Patricia Plattner

On 28 March 1996, the Glasgow Film Theatre, in an event associated with the Conference *25 Years Emancipation? Women in Switzerland 1971– 1996*, screened two Swiss films (*Joe and Marie*, 1994, directed by Tania Stöcklin, and *Piano Panier*, 1989, directed by Patricia Plattner). Patricia Plattner, who was present for the screening, commented on her career as a film director and answered questions from the audience. The interview with Patricia Plattner published here was conducted by Joy Charnley, Malcolm Pender and Andrew Wilkin at the University of Strathclyde on 29 March 1996.

Joy Charnley: I thought we could start with some background on how you started out in cinema. Are there any family connections? Is there anyone in your family connected with the arts or with cinema?

Patricia Plattner: Connected with the arts? Yes, a little bit. I had an uncle who was a sculptor, but otherwise no. I am from scientific people, my father is a doctor in Geneva.

Joy Charnley: You said last night that when you started out you thought it was very difficult.

Patricia Plattner: I always wanted to do something in the arts and so, well, I hesitated, – architecture, history of art, cinema. Cinema seemed very complicated, and so I decided I had to go away, but it was a bit difficult financially. So I decided to stay in Geneva and do the Ecole des Beaux Arts as well as history of art at the University. I took both. The Ecole des Beaux Arts was changing at that time, just into the 1970s. It began to be not only a traditional school of art, but also interested in new media like photography and video and things like that. So I did my diploma there in mixed media, as we called it at that time. Just after I left they created a new section for cinema and audio–visual art, because there had been a couple of us who hoped that they would develop that part of the school.

JOY CHARNLEY: And so it was developed just a bit later then?

PATRICIA PLATTNER: We were the starters, but we left the school when it was created, and now there is a section in the Ecole des Beaux Arts which has another name. It's called the Superior School of Visual Arts or something like that, so now they have a section where one can study cinema, but it's not really a film school, because they don't have a lot of material. But they have history of cinema and can make little films.

JOY CHARNLEY: You said last night that it was in 1983 when you started getting involved.

PATRICIA PLATTNER: Yes, because I finished university in 1975, then I did paintings and some performance art and video art. Then I went to Canada as Artist in Residence where I did video.

ANDREW WILKIN: Where were you in Canada?

PATRICIA PLATTNER: In Vancouver. It was in 1982 or something like that. A friend of mine asked me to be art director for his film. I decided straight away to do it because he hadn't studied cinema. It was his first film.

JOY CHARNLEY: You thought, if he can do it, then ...

PATRICIA PLATTNER: I thought that if he can do it, then I can do it too.

MALCOLM PENDER: Had you, in your youth, gone a lot to the cinema?

PATRICIA PLATTNER: I liked cinema a lot. But I've never been a movie fan who would go every day. But I've always liked it, and maybe it was also because I like to write, I like music, I like painting. It's an art where I can use many things that I love, and also, since I finished school, I have shared a studio with two other people, two other friends, and I like team work. I like to be in a group. The side I knew less was probably the acting side, but I felt quite at ease with framing and editing and things like that because one also uses those when painting.

JOY CHARNLEY: In a sense you got into it by chance because you said if this person can do it, then perhaps I could as well. Would you say that it's not as difficult as it looks? Have you found it perhaps less difficult than some people might assume?

PATRICIA PLATTNER: The more I go on, the more I find it difficult. Cinema is a very difficult art, I think, and you have to know a lot of things. The more you are on the inside of it, the more you feel you don't know much, because you have to know a lot of things and you need to have a lot of ability for many different things. But it's true that, if you know about it, and I think I have always known about it a bit, you can also choose the right people to work with you. For example, a good cameraman, if you can talk with him, he can explain a lot of things to you. The sound man can also do the same for you. You cannot know everything. The editor will contribute something for you. It's really a job where many people are working together and collaborating.

MALCOLM PENDER: It seemed to me, from something you said last night, when you said that you've got to be pragmatic, that that was the essential difference between, say, writing a book, where you are sitting determining exactly what happens, and making a film, where to some extent you are dependent on chance elements, such as who is available, what is available in terms of money, and so on, and the chance elements have a larger influence on a film than they would on a book.

PATRICIA PLATTNER: Exactly.

JOY CHARNLEY: Have you had help from film-makers in Switzerland or outside of Switzerland, perhaps as role models, as examples, as mentors?

PATRICIA PLATTNER: There were people around me who were cameramen or similar. I met literary people. For instance I met Alain Tanner.

JOY CHARNLEY: There have been comparisons drawn with Tanner and Soutter.

PATRICIA PLATTNER: Well, we come from the same city and it's true that perhaps there is a common background. They are much older than I am. Soutter died a few years ago, and Tanner must be in his late sixties, so we are really a generation after. But I met him when I was hesitating whether to set up a production company with a friend. He wanted to become a producer and I dislike the job of production, but as I'm pragmatic, I also know a little bit about how to do it. So at the beginning we started out like that, thinking that a few years later he would take care of the production side and I would be able to make my films inside that structure. But then he went to work at Swiss television and now he is one of the chiefs of Swiss television. We realised that it was very difficult – I mean to produce films – and we lost a lot of money. It's very risky, so at the time I was wondering whether to keep that little company, because it's burdensome having a limited company. But you need to, because you have so much money in hand. I was alone and I was hesitating. Then I spoke to Tanner because I noticed that he had always kept his company, and he encouraged me to keep mine if I could, because he told me that later – and it's true that I have the rights and all my negatives – it would be important when I had to take a decision. So Tanner encouraged me and told me to try and keep it as long as I could.

JOY CHARNLEY: Apart from that specific instance, there wasn't much networking to speak of?

PATRICIA PLATTNER: No. You know, it's a small country and the older ones don't like us too much because there are a lot of us now, and there isn't any more money than before, so they receive less money than twenty years ago.

ANDREW WILKIN: Have you been interested in films from France, Germany or Italy previously? Any directors in particular?

PATRICIA PLATTNER: Of course. I love Italian cinema mostly. Antonioni and all his neo-realist films were really among my favourites. I also liked Wenders at the beginning, but I like him less now. French cinema, maybe less. Well, I liked Rohmer and some Godard, but really I liked them more at the beginning of the *nouvelle vague* in the 1960s.

JOY CHARNLEY: One thing I was reading in relation to Switzerland was this issue of people who stay rooted in an area. Last night you mentioned the actress who has remained in Portugal and the difficulties subsequently of getting work. Have you been tempted to move to Paris, for example? For your career, do you think that would be a good move?

PATRICIA PLATTNER: Yes, I have been tempted, but it would be difficult, I think. I am in a better position staying in Switzerland than moving to Paris now. I travel a lot. I go to Paris virtually once a month, and when I am preparing for a film or something like that, even every week. It is three hours by train. It's easier for me to say I'm a Swiss film-maker – and sometimes I can bring some money there – than to be among all the other French film-makers. So maybe if once I make a good film, a successful film, I could really spend my time between Paris and Geneva, with a little apartment in Paris. But what I do now is just go and sleep at friends', and I don't even have a phone number, but that's what all the Swiss do.

JOY CHARNLEY: Your identity as a *Swiss* film-maker, you don't mind that?

PATRICIA PLATTNER: No. I just mind it a little bit because it's difficult, it's really difficult when you want to show your film in France. You are Swiss. You are provincial. It's much more difficult for us. For instance, little things like accents. It's not really a French problem, it's Parisian. I'm sure that a film-maker in Marseilles or Lyons has the same problems as we have. It's really this problem of Paris.

MALCOLM PENDER: But, on the other hand, the Swiss market couldn't sustain you commercially.

PATRICIA PLATTNER: It's impossible, because the French-speaking part of Switzerland is something like one million eight hundred thousand people. It's nothing! The Swiss-Germans, they can, because they are more important, so if one of their films is successful in the Swiss-German part, they can consider that they have a market.

JOY CHARNLEY: What about links with German-speaking Switzerland? Again, you suggested last night that it was perhaps a bit difficult.

PATRICIA PLATTNER: It is very difficult. But the film *Piano Panier*, for instance, worked well in the Swiss-German part. I don't know why, but maybe it was ... Well, maybe the humour. Maybe the French tone. I don't know. Probably it was a bit exotic for them, *and* Swiss, so they were happy. But we cannot show most of our films. It's very difficult. We always try of course, we always try.

ANDREW WILKIN: What about the Arts Council Pro Helvetia? Have they always helped you?

PATRICIA PLATTNER: It's very complicated because they have to cover all the arts and cinema as well. But there is a separate section for cinema because we need much more money, so there is a cinema section just for us. At Pro Helvetia they represent us and send some films to Embassies, or sometimes to Conferences like this one in Glasgow. They have no money at all for cinema production at Pro Helvetia.

ANDREW WILKIN: How do you get commercial money for production?

PATRICIA PLATTNER: We don't get commercial money. We have another government-funded cultural department where we get special funding for cinema. But we don't get commercial money. We have television money which we can consider as commercial because they are also involved in production, otherwise it's nearly all state or foundation money.

MALCOLM PENDER: But it's quite difficult putting it together. I noticed in the literature I read about *Piano Panier* and from what you said last night that you got money from the Ville de Genève and from a variety of sources. Asking for the money is tremendously complicated and time-consuming.

PATRICIA PLATTNER: Yes, as I said before, it's rather a burdensome task. At the beginning I tried writing to a hundred addresses, but I noticed that there were only between five and ten which worked. So now I don't write a hundred letters. Now I go to these ten people and try to defend my project.

JOY CHARNLEY: Have the distribution problems and the money situation improved since you started?

PATRICIA PLATTNER: Yes.

MALCOLM PENDER: Is that partly because you're better known now?

PATRICIA PLATTNER: Well, I'm a bit known!

ANDREW WILKIN: You're too modest! If *Piano Panier* was the first *long métrage*, and there have been other films since then, as well as other *court métrage* films beforehand, there has been time for you to develop.

PATRICIA PLATTNER: I must say that since *Piano Panier* I have only been working in cinema. Before, I still had my graphics to do and I was still a graphic designer probably four days per week, whilst one day a week I was working for the cinema. Now it's the opposite. Sometimes for three days a month I do a poster, because it's a theatre company I like, and I like to find my pencils and do it for the pleasure and for a change. But since 1988–1989 I have put all my energy into making films and into co-producing some. I've found some money for films in French.

ANDREW WILKIN: Can we ask you about what is loosely called in English the 'Woman Question'? Since last night we've spoken to a number of people and they've all uniformly said that they thoroughly enjoyed the film, and thought it was very accurate in the portrayal from a woman's point of view.

JOY CHARNLEY: Yes, I was wondering how you felt about being almost put in the pigeon-hole of 'woman director'. People like Coline Serreau and Diane Kurys have said 'I'm not a woman director. I'm a director.'

MALCOLM PENDER: Yes, that's right. Someone said at one point that *Piano Panier* is very obviously a woman's film. Why is it? It wasn't obvious to me, I have to say, although I enjoyed the film enormously.

PATRICIA PLATTNER: But it's true that *Piano Panier* is a woman's film. I don't think a man could have written the story like that. But, for instance, in another film I made, *The Crystal Book*, there is a totally different point of view because my hero is a man. There the main character is a man and the story is seen through the eyes of a man, so I don't want to be a 'woman director'. Moreover, the three documentary portraits I have done were on men. If I were really a 'woman director', I would have chosen a woman writer. No, that's not really my objective. I do what I feel like doing, when I want.

JOY CHARNLEY: But at the same time you can say things about women that maybe men directors couldn't. I think that the reaction of several people to your film shows that it is an accurate portrayal of friendship.

PATRICIA PLATTNER: Exactly. Of course, in that sense I think I have a woman's sensibilities and I am a woman in the way that I direct my films. I am sure that relationships on stage are very different with technicians and so on. You are as you are.

JOY CHARNLEY: In *Piano Panier* you imply a certain attitude to Switzerland. Somebody mentioned it and you yourself also said that it was a question of North and South. It made me think it was a bit like the Georges Haldas book *La maison en Calabre*, which is again Switzerland, but Switzerland-Italy. Was that in your mind? Was that something you wanted to do in this film? Was that something you feel about Switzerland?

PATRICIA PLATTNER: Yes, I do feel it. In Geneva, for instance, where I live – in a district called Carouge, in the 1950s and 1960s there was a lot of Italian immigration, and they brought a lot of things to the life there. Where I live there were a lot of Italians, but little by little they went back home. We had the Spanish people coming in the 1970s, and then in the 1980s the Portuguese. The Spanish are the ones who have stayed. They are now *petits bourgeois,* and whilst most of the Italians who had come in the 1950s and 1960s went back home, their children stayed, but they now feel Swiss. So in my everyday life, where I go to drink my coffee, I am confronted by these people. I have had a lot of Portuguese people in my house.

MALCOLM PENDER: One of the things in your film that fascinated me was the notion of family. It seemed to be portrayed as a southern thing, because Marie kept saying that she had no family, and then she was utterly surprised that her friend should go back to a notion of family. Towards the end you saw her being integrated, and yet she wasn't fully integrated to the extent that she was sitting outside playing a piano. Do you get that from your own direct experience?

PATRICIA PLATTNER: No, no, not at all, because I come from a very large family. In my father's family there were twelve children, in my mother's four. There are five of us in my family. We come from the mountains and we are Swiss Catholic, so we are more Latin. So with the kids of my age I noticed that some friends of mine are only children.

MALCOLM PENDER: The other thing that struck me – and for me this was the most fascinating aspect of the film – was the pace of the film. I thought that was beautiful and wanted to ask you how you did this. Here you have a story where nothing sensational happens and, in fact, you don't really have much of a continuous plot at all. There is discontinuity built into the plot and the problem is to sustain the interest of the viewer in this. I wondered if the editing was extremely important in this? I began to notice that the scenes you were presenting didn't last a terribly long period of time. Is this an important element?

PATRICIA PLATTNER: That was already there in the writing, because I remember that when I was writing, I decided to work more on short features. Each time I was constructing a sequence, I had one sequence and then another one, and they all had more or less the same pace, the same number of lines. It's true that the editing is well done. I was surprised to see it again.

JOY CHARNLEY: Is it the first time you've seen the film again for a few years?

PATRICIA PLATTNER: For four years, I think.

JOY CHARNLEY: Was it a nice surprise to see it again?

PATRICIA PLATTNER: Part of it I liked, and part of it I didn't. It was OK.

ANDREW WILKIN: You wrote the script for *Piano Panier* yourself. Did you write the scripts for your more recent films?

PATRICIA PLATTNER: For the documentaries, yes. But for *The Crystal Book* the script came from a short story by the Swiss writer Claude Delarue. At the beginning I wrote on my own, but then I found some money to work with a French scriptwriter in Paris, and I did a second or third version with him. After that, I got some money from the European Script Fund in London to work with another scriptwriter, this time a British scriptwriter, in London. After that I was able to raise the production money and just before shooting I did another six versions of the script on my own. In the end we co-signed. There are three authors to the manuscript – the Frenchman, the Englishman, and myself.

ANDREW WILKIN: You know that in the course of the next two and a half days we are going to be looking at the period since 1971, and particularly from the point of view of the change of experience for women in Switzerland over that time. What is your impression of these last twenty-five years?

PATRICIA PLATTNER: I think many things have changed.

MALCOLM PENDER: For the better?

PATRICIA PLATTNER: For the better. I remember well when I started, because it was 1971. At the art school and university I remember that one of my teachers said to me: 'I hope you are not one of those women who come here at 10 o'clock and leave at 11.30 to go and do the cooking for your husband'. I always had the feeling during my studies that I had to work ten times harder to prove that I really wanted that life as a student.

JOY CHARNLEY: They were expecting you to take it very seriously?

PATRICIA PLATTNER: Yes, because even at the Art School we were two-thirds girls and one-third boys, and yet the one-third of boys were considered seriously – they had really chosen to be artists. The girls – they were expected to be married or doing Art School because they liked to paint a little bit. That was a bit difficult, I think, at the beginning of my work, because I really wanted to do it professionally, and I always had the feeling that I had to work harder. But why not?

MALCOLM PENDER: Do you think that's not the case now for somebody coming in?

PATRICIA PLATTNER: It's changed a little bit. Maybe it's also because after ten years, given that I have done quite a lot of things, I am taken more seriously. I don't know.

JOY CHARNLEY: Have you got personal memories of 1971, of the introduction of the vote?

PATRICIA PLATTNER: I remember it well. I was just eighteen, and for me it was the moment when I could go and vote. It was good timing. It's true that we were very offended, but we fought for it, I remember, as teenagers. I really wanted to be among those persons who could vote. It's quite impressive now to think that only twenty-five years have passed.

ANDREW WILKIN: What does the future hold for you?

PATRICIA PLATTNER: I'm working on a documentary now, one I shot in Abyssinia. It's a lot of work because I came back with eleven hours of images and twenty hours of interviews, so it's a big editing job. After that, I have another documentary that I have to do for Swiss television, a shorter one, and less complicated, and that will take me up to the end of 1996. I would very much like to do another feature film, but the situation now is economically very difficult, because people don't believe in that kind of film any more, because we spend a million pounds in any event and there is no return, so it is a bit frustrating.

JOY CHARNLEY: Do you feel that maybe money is not being put into things like art and culture, but into other things?

PATRICIA PLATTNER: Well, they have cut back on the best things, and now they only want to support films which will be successful. As with a radio script, they say there is no suspense, no action, and yet those are films that I don't want to do. I'm not interested. I prefer to do a good documentary the way I like.

MALCOLM PENDER: This is where public money presumably becomes as restrictive as commercial money. Commercial money only wants a return, so it's going to recycle things that have had returns in the past.

PATRICIA PLATTNER: But even now the government is trying to give some help. If your film turns out to be a success, they give you more money. It's a sort of reward.

JOY CHARNLEY: You get rewarded for success, but you have to have success in the first place before they'll start to reward you.

PATRICIA PLATTNER: But I know I will write another one. The last one was a very big film, the one I shot in Sri Lanka. It was expensive, not by British standards, but for Switzerland expensive.

JOY CHARNLEY: How much is expensive in Swiss terms?

PATRICIA PLATTNER: One million two hundred thousand pounds, something like that. *Piano Panier* was two hundred and fifty thousand.

ANDREW WILKIN: It's certainly a big jump.

PATRICIA PLATTNER: It was a big jump, and it was a big film with a large crew, quite difficult, but I like it.

JOY CHARNLEY: Are you quite pessimistic about Swiss cinema?

PATRICIA PLATTNER: A bit pessimistic, yes.

JOY CHARNLEY: You were saying, however, that there is another generation coming up.

PATRICIA PLATTNER: A lot of young people. I hope they will do something. But I hardly know anybody who is writing scripts because there is such a mess at this time. It's very difficult to go to work and believe in something. Now there are all these talks on how to get more money, and what the government will do. Television is also harder than even five years ago because they put our films on at one o'clock in the morning, and then say they don't want to give money except for prime-time film. They want us to produce popular films for television, because they are all looking at numbers, at how many people are viewing. For me that's another business. I'm not a director for television.

ANDREW WILKIN: Have any of your films been shown on British television?

PATRICIA PLATTNER: Unfortunately not.

ANDREW WILKIN: Yet just recently, at one o'clock in the morning, I saw on TV a Swiss-Italian film, just over one hour in length, called *La Signora in verde*. It was on Channel 4, it was an extremely good film, and it had been purchased specifically. They made an important statement that this was a Swiss product, not French, German, or Italian, but Swiss. But you haven't had any sales on British television thus far?

PATRICIA PLATTNER: No. But it's true that the shelf-life of a film can be rather long. Either you sell it very quickly, when it is on show at a festival, and they push it then, or they wait two years, three years, sometimes four years, and then they can buy it for less and they have all these hours to fill.

ANDREW WILKIN: Have you been to any film festivals this year? Did you go to Locarno just recently?

PATRICIA PLATTNER: Yes, of course. My second film was in competition at Locarno two years ago, and that was interesting because we were three Swiss women directors in competition. Before the Festival, there were big headlines 'three women directors', including Tania Stöcklin and myself, but the journalists, the Swiss-Germans especially, said 'these women, they don't know how to make films'. It was really a macho reaction, very macho.

ANDREW WILKIN: Did you have anything at Solothurn this year? That was recent as well.

PATRICIA PLATTNER: Each time I make a film, it is at Solothurn, because that's a window for Swiss film. No, I was happy to have the two films in competition at Locarno, but the last one I nearly regretted because – as they say – 'you cannot be a prophet in your own country'. Maybe it would have been better for me to go to Venice.

JOY CHARNLEY: Again you have the Swiss label, as it were.

PATRICIA PLATTNER: It's a small country, and you have a lot of jealousy, and you know how it is.

ANDREW WILKIN: We must say that one of the striking features we have thought of for this weekend is precisely the fact that Switzerland and Scotland are of similar proportions and quite similar population as well. There is a very thriving artistic world in Scotland of course, and very recently we have seen films that have been winning Oscars and so forth, which is encouraging, so things can be done out of small countries. One of the things that has attracted us in a literary context is precisely the fact that we are operating out of a small country and are concerned with a small country.

JOY CHARNLEY: Then there are the references you made to Sri Lanka and Thailand – clearly a wider stage – the world-wide thing is something that you are interested in. It's quite important for you.

PATRICIA PLATTNER: It's quite important for me. It's important for Tanner, who is a French-Swiss. He also has a place in Spain. I think we live in a country which we sometimes need to leave.

MALCOLM PENDER: But it's interesting to see that in a movement, because there are quite a lot of well known and epoch-making documentaries in the 1970s set in Switzerland, but now they've moved out with your generation. It was the older generation who were making them in the 1970s, but your generation is moving out.

PATRICIA PLATTNER: But now I think they are coming back in.

JOY CHARNLEY: You don't think that in the near future you'll be inspired by a Swiss topic?

PATRICIA PLATTNER: The documentary, which I will do for Swiss television after the present one, will be a documentary set around Mont Blanc, because there you have three valleys. You have a Swiss valley, a French valley with Chamonix, and an Italian one with Val d'Aosta. That's in part my subject, to see that we have three countries but the same population around this mountain. They have a common language, a *patois*, a dialect, a common history, and common music. I think your country is little, but it's not the boundaries we know. Sometimes it's more where you like.

Joy Charnley: Rather than being the boundaries which have been drawn on a map?

Patricia Plattner: Exactly. Because, for instance, I'm sure that Geneva is closer to Lyons than to Zürich. You have the Rhône, the mentality, the architecture, and so forth. So I find it interesting.

Andrew Wilkin: Well, I think we must draw to a close here. So, Patricia, can we say thank you very much to you for having spent some time with us telling us about your work. Thank you very much indeed.

ELISABETTA PAGNOSSIN ALIGISAKIS

The Current Status of Women in Political Life: Women and Politics in Switzerland since 1971

It is not very easy to describe briefly the situation of Swiss women in the political sphere. In order to do so, I shall focus on two axes: political culture and the representation of women in political institutions. A limited number of indicators will permit me to outline the relationship 'women and politics in Switzerland' from a comparative and diachronic view.

One of the significant traits of the Swiss political system is federalism. This characteristic is also a determining feature when one analyses the introduction of women's political rights in the country. Not all Swiss women have been able to practise those rights simultaneously at both cantonal and federal levels. In fact, in 1971, Swiss men granted their fellow-citizens the right to vote and to be elected at the federal level. By the same date, women only in certain cantons were already enfranchised at the cantonal level.

This relatively recent introduction of women's political rights is remarkable from several points of view. In a traditionally democratic country, where men had enjoyed such rights for more than a century, the principle of equality between men and women in the political sphere was recognised much later than in other countries. Thus Switzerland was the penultimate European country to grant women political equality – the last being Liechtenstein in 1984!

In 1971, the initiative proposing political equality at the federal level was accepted by two-thirds (65.7 per cent) of the electors and by twenty-two cantons (and demi-cantons), although in a few cantons it was only narrowly accepted. Subsequently, in the following two years, most Swiss women also obtained political rights at the cantonal level. Two demi-cantons, however, still resisted this egalitarian move. Moreover, whilst within Appenzell Outer Rhodes electors granted political rights to women in 1989, it was the Federal Tribunal which had to impose female political equality on Appenzell Inner Rhodes in 1990, with this decision being based on the article on equality between men and women inserted in the Constitution in 1981.

Clearly, from a formally legal point of view, the political integration of women in Switzerland is relatively recent. This does not mean that women were not participating in the world of politics by being, for instance, members of political parties and of trade unions. Nonetheless, it remains difficult to ascertain with precision the exact consequences that resulted from the absence of long experience of formal democratic practice.

Let us now turn to the situation of women in Swiss political culture. It should be emphasised that the political culture of any country is characterised by the opinions, attitudes and behaviour patterns of the majority of the entire population, men and women. These characteristics influence choices that are made. In other words, it is probably not a mere coincidence that female Swiss citizens obtained their political rights so late!

A number of indicators could be analysed in order to point out certain traits of Swiss political culture. Of course, each of these indicators explains only partially the political culture. To start with, let us examine the right to vote, which is often considered, rightly or wrongly, as the minimum level on the scale of political participation of the individual. The will and the opportunity to be elected, considered as the top level on the same scale, will be dealt with in the second part of the present contribution.

A study concerning the right to vote was conducted among the Swiss electorate in 1972. It revealed that, during the first federal elections in which women were able to participate, only half (49 per cent) of the female citizens questioned had actually voted, compared to almost three-quarters (72 per cent) of men.[1] At subsequent elections, the levels of electoral participation of men and women grew closer. Indeed, whilst the percentage difference had been 20 points at the National Council elections of 1971, twenty years later it fell to 11 percentage points.[2]

---

1 Ronald Inglehart and Dusan Sidjanski, 'Electeurs et dimension gauche-droite', in Dusan Sidjanski et al., *Les Suisses et la politique. Enquête sur les attitudes d'électeurs suisses (1972)* (Berne: H. Lang, 1975), pp. 83–124 (p. 90).
2 Thanh-Huyen Ballmer-Cao, Katharina Belser, and Elisabeth Keller, 'La lente percée des femmes dans les parlements et dans les gouvernements', in Commission Fédérale pour les Questions Féminines, *Des acquis – mais peu de changements? La situation des femmes en Suisse* (Berne: 1995), pp. 47–57 (pp. 55–56).

In Switzerland, which is a highly participatory democracy, citizens are often requested to give their opinion on a variety of subjects, based on popular initiatives or on referenda proposed by the State authorities. These are not the same issues, however, which are at stake in such voting procedures as is the case when electing political representatives. Nonetheless, even in the context of such opinion-casting, one can detect a margin (albeit slightly less significant than in the context of elections) between the percentage participation of men and women. Some figures may serve to illustrate this. From 1977 to 1983 the participation of men in voting was, on average, 11 percentage points higher than that for women. From 1984 to 1991 the difference decreased to approximately 10 percentage points. Then, finally, during the popular votes held in 1991 and 1992 the difference went down to 8 points.[3]

Thus, it could be concluded that the indicator based on male and female participation rates in popular voting and in elections shows that the gap still exists, but that it is diminishing with time. In other words, women vote less than men, but with time their number increases.

Let us take the example of another indicator of political culture, namely the lack of preference for a particular political party, as a sign of a certain detachment and disinterest in political matters. Two pieces of research can help us to trace the evolution of this indicator. The first, undertaken in 1972, reveals that approximately one-fifth (22 per cent) of male electors and two-fifths (41 per cent) of female electors had no preference for a particular political party.[4] The second, concerning the equivalent figures for Switzerland in 1988–89, shows that, 18 years after the earlier research, the lack of preference for a given party was recorded by approximately one-third (34 per cent) of the male voters and almost half (49 per cent) of the female voters.[5] So the percentage difference between men and women in terms of party preference has decreased from 19 points to 15 points, evincing a tendency to rapprochement. At the same time, there

---

3 ibid.
4 Henri Kerr, 'Electeurs et forces partisanes', in D. Sidjanski et al., *Les Suisses et la politique,* op. cit., pp. 45–82 (p. 53).
5 Elisabetta Pagnossin Aligisakis, in 'Localisme versus cosmopolitisme. Les attitudes politiques des Suissesses', Contribution présentée lors du Congrès de l'Association Suisse de Science Politique, 13–14 novembre 1992, Balsthal, 51 pp. (p. 15).

can be noted an increase in the number of men who do not identify with any party (+12 points). Thus, to analyse in a simple dichotomous manner between men and women could, in the long run, cause errors, especially if one uses the male group as the main element in the comparison, neglecting other elements such as socio-economic standing, level of education, and age. If there are differences within the female group, it is true that analysis also reveals differences between female voters and male voters as groups. These differences can only partially be attributed to the late exercise of women's political rights. For the present contributor these differences are caused by several factors which can be found in the political culture of the country, and in the transmission of this culture through the traditionally different identification of men and women in terms of social and political roles. In other words, the private domain is reserved for women, and the public domain, which includes politics, is reserved for men. From this separation of operating spheres and roles derive, theoretically, the apolitical attitude of women and the absence of political roles for women.

In order to recognise the part played by citizens, both male and female, who continue to conform to the traditional separation of political roles, let us now examine some forms of political behaviour and attitudes. To start with, it must be borne in mind that, in 1971, almost a third of the (then exclusively male) electors were opposed to equal political rights for women at the federal level. For them, politics had to remain 'men's business'! Ten years later, in 1981, 40 per cent of the electors refused to accept the law on equality between men and women, even though women were more in favour of it than men (+14 percentage points).[6] These figures show that a significant part of the Swiss population (both male and female) refused the possibility, just 15 years ago, that women could enjoy, on the basis of equality, the same social and political roles as men. Moreover, according to other research carried out, this traditional separation of roles seems still to have been significant in 1988 for a part of the Swiss population. Thus it was that more

---

6 Claude Longchamps, 'Etude comparative du comportement électoral des femmes et des hommes (1971–1988)', in Commission Fédérale pour les Questions Féminines, *Prenez place, Madame. La représentation politique des femmes en Suisse* (Berne: mai 1990), pp. 117–165 (p. 158).

than half (54 per cent) of those persons questioned agreed 'fully' (21 per cent) or 'partially' (33 per cent) with the statement that women are by nature more averse to politics than men.[7] According to the same study, almost 15 per cent of Swiss men and women were convinced of male intellectual superiority. Indeed, both men and women agreed with the idea that, compared with women, men had greater abilities.[8] Moreover, almost a quarter of the persons questioned agreed with the statement that women are too emotional, immoderate, and not very rational in dealing with facts.[9] Clearly, the old stereotype of the 'weaker sex' (both physically and intellectually) had not yet disappeared! A relatively significant portion of the Swiss population at large still shared attitudes and behaviours that reflected a very traditional political culture.

The idea that politics should be 'men's business' was also common, however, within the twelve member States of the European Community.[10] In 1987, more than one-fifth of men (23 per cent) and women (21 per cent) shared this conviction, compared with one-third of men (36 per cent) and women (31 per cent) in the Europe of the Nine in 1975. If, with time, the openness to women in the political world has accelerated, important differences continued to be identified among people of different age groups, levels of education, political options and member States. Without doubt, however, by the end of the 1980s, this trait of traditional political culture was still much more firmly rooted in Switzerland than in the countries of the Europe of the Twelve.

Let us continue this comparison between Switzerland and the Community countries by analysing two other indicators of political culture: the lack of interest in politics, and the frequency of political discussions. By the end of the 1980s, during a survey on values in Switzerland, a quarter of men (25 per cent) and more than a third of women (37 per cent) admitted their lack of interest in politics. Similar data which existed for the Europe of the Twelve revealed that the lack of interest

---

7 Regula Stämpfli, 'Attitudes à l'égard des mesures destinées à promouvoir les femmes lors des élections au Conseil National', in *Prenez place, Madame*, op. cit., pp. 169–214 (pp. 201 and 210).
8 ibid., pp. 203 and 210.
9 ibid., pp. 204 and 210.
10 Elisabetta Pagnossin Aligisakis, op. cit.

in politics declared by Swiss men and women was much higher than that declared by male (16 per cent) and female (29 per cent) citizens of the European Community. But, and on the contrary, the lack of political discussions was rarer in Switzerland than in the twelve member States of the European Community. In fact, 15 per cent of Swiss men and 24 per cent of Swiss women said they never participated in political discussions, compared to 27 per cent of men and 40 per cent of women in the European Community. Clearly, the difference is more significant for women (+16 percentage points). What is most surprising is the difference between the proportion of Swiss people who do not have an interest in politics and the relatively low proportion of those who never have political discussions.

The question which arises, therefore, is whether, when analysing in a more detailed manner, and by combining the two above-mentioned indicators, there are major differences between the level of political integration of Swiss women and that of women in the Community countries. Apparently not. For the purposes of comparison, we could divide the twelve European Community countries into two groups, taking into consideration simultaneously the indicator of interest in politics and that of political discussions. By doing so, we can produce the following classification. A first group of countries includes, in decreasing order of female politicisation, Denmark, Germany, Luxembourg, the Netherlands, the United Kingdom, France and Greece. In this group, the politicisation of women seems to be relatively high. A second group comprises Ireland, Belgium, Spain, Italy and Portugal, where women's distance from politics remains significant. Ireland is on the borderline in this classification, with almost one-third of women questioned showing no interest at all in politics, and fewer than half of them never discussing political matters.

The Swiss data concerning the indicator of interest in politics are close to those of Ireland. On the other hand, when considering the frequency of political discussions, the Swiss data are close to those for Denmark, a country with a reputation for being progressive on issues of equality.

The integration of Swiss women into the political world, whilst incomplete, is at a high average position compared to that of women in the twelve countries of the European Community. The differences which still exist between men and women, in terms of political integration, are systematically decreasing when the factors of age and level of education are taken into consideration to amend the apparent homogeneity of these two groups defined by their sex.

Political options are often measured on a left-right scale. From the study on values in Switzerland,[11] it can be seen that the expression of self-positioning at the extreme poles of the scale were identical for persons of both sexes. The only differences extracted from the opinions given by such persons are an orientation towards the centre which is more significant among women than among men (which could mask indecisiveness), as well as a right-wing option which is more noticeable among men. Other researches confirm these results. Female conservatism, documented in the past, seems to be nothing but a memory in Switzerland, as in other countries. Nonetheless, the incapacity to position oneself on a left-right scale (in other words to retain a political option) is higher in women (29 per cent) than it is in men (14 per cent).[12] Apart from this observation, differences of behaviour between men and women in their choice of the options proposed when voting are slight. In other words, one does not vote differently as a result of being a man or a woman, but rather other determinants condition the choice of the whole Swiss population when facing the options proposed. Even when the voting concerns a matter that touches women more directly, other than for a slight increase in the number of female voters, there is no major difference allied to sex in the choice of the option voted for.[13]

In brief, two conclusions could be inferred from the first part of this contribution. Firstly, the lack of political integration is still more significant for women than for men. Yet, with time, the tendency towards a male-female reconciliation for all the indicators is confirmed. Secondly, women who are more integrated into the political world (and

11 Elisabetta Pagnossin Aligisakis, 'Le rôle social et politique des femmes: quels changements?', in A. Melich, ed., *Les valeurs en Suisse* (Berne: Lang, 1991), pp. 337–388.

12 ibid., pp. 360–362.

13 Guilhermina Marques de Bastos, 'La sélectivité de la participation', in H. Kriesi, ed., *Citoyenneté et démocratie directe. Compétence, participation et décision des citoyens et citoyennes suisses* (Zürich: Seismo, 1993), pp. 167–188.

who are characterised by a relatively high socio-economic status) generally choose in a manner similar to that of men. Thus it can be demonstrated that there is no real difference in the choices of men and
women, either in Switzerland or in other countries.

Let us now deal with the second part of this analysis – the evolution
of female political representation at the federal and cantonal levels. In
the space of 25 years, the proportion of female representation in the National Council has increased at a slow but continuous rate, passing from
5 per cent in 1971 to 21.5 per cent in 1995. The number of women
elected to the National Council is relatively high compared to the number of women elected to the lower or single chambers of the Parliaments
of other European countries. Compared with the member States of the
European Union, in terms of this indicator, Switzerland was headed in
1995 by Sweden (40.4 per cent), Finland (33.5 per cent), Denmark (33
per cent), the Netherlands (31.3 per cent), Germany (26.2 per cent) and
Austria (23.5 per cent).[14]

The presence of women in the lower or single chambers of Parliaments was proportionately less in Greece (6 per cent), France (6.4 per
cent), Portugal (8.7 per cent) and the United Kingdom (9.5 per cent)
than it was in Switzerland! Neither in these countries, nor in Switzerland, does the date of introduction of women's political rights seem to
be a determining factor. This is indeed remarkable. Despite the fact that
women started the exercise of their political rights rather late in Switzerland, the proportion of women elected has been achieved rather
quickly. The electoral system applied in Switzerland for the election of
the 200 deputies of the National Council is often invoked. This system is a proportional representation system within which each canton
constitutes an electoral district with a different number of seats reserved
to be filled (the seats are proportional to the resident cantonal population, with the minimum number of cantonal seats being one). The proportional representation system seems to favour the election of women
because of the depersonalisation of the electoral competition which
takes place and, in addition, because of the larger electoral constituencies used. These two characteristics of the electoral system implemented

14 Union Interparlementaire, *Les femmes dans les Parlements, 1945–1995. Etude statistique mondiale*, Série 'Rapports et documents', n° 23 (Geneva: 1995).

in Switzerland are not sufficient, however, to explain the better representation of women from a comparative point of view. To start with, it should not be forgotten that in Switzerland the system used for the expression of preferences by the electorate (implemented by means of the possibility of voting on the same ticket for candidates belonging to different party lists, and the concurrence of the name of a candidate on these same lists) offers the electors many possibilities to choose one particular candidate among several others. Analyses conducted in other countries indicate that voters are less hesitant to choose female candidates than political parties are to put forward female candidates when electoral lists are being prepared. The second advantage of the proportional representation system is that the electoral constituencies are larger. Because of this fact, female candidates are given further advantage since there is less conflict as several seats are to be filled. Moreover, the proportion of votes needed to be elected is lower than in the case of more restricted electoral constituencies.

Currently, the Council of States (composed of 46 members representing the cantons) is elected under the simple majority system (other than for the canton of Jura). As is the case in most upper chambers of other European countries, the evolution of female representation has been discontinuous and weaker than that in the lower chambers. Nevertheless, in 1995 female representation reached 17.4 per cent with eight women being elected. That being said, the explanation for the greater number of women elected under the proportional representation system is apparently attractive, but only partially satisfying. The political representation of women in other countries which apply the same electoral system is lower. That does not exclude influences linked to institutional factors, such as technical elements permitted in electoral systems which determine party strategies as well as the range of choice offered to the electorate. The party affiliation of women elected and candidates presented seems to be a much more interesting explanation.

Female representation in the Swiss National Council following the latest elections is greatest among the Greens, where women constitute the majority (69 per cent, with 6 women out of 10 seats gained). In the Socialist Party it reaches 35 per cent (19 women out of 54 seats). Among the governing 'bourgeois' parties, the Radical Democratic Party has strongly increased its female presence to 18 per cent of the elected members (8 women out of 54 seats). In the Christian Democratic Party women account for 15 per cent of the deputies (5 out of 34), and for 10 per cent in the Democratic Union of the Centre (3 out of 29 seats). Extreme right-wing parties have never had any women elected.[15]

It is pertinent to take a brief look at the origins of the women elected in terms of the linguistic regions from which they come. Currently, this aspect is often important in explaining certain cultural differences within Switzerland. For example, in 1995, not one woman from Ticino was elected to the National Council, despite the fact that women constituted 15.9 per cent of the candidates on the electoral lists in the canton. Yet again it was confirmed that the preponderance of women elected were from German-speaking Switzerland. They represent a quarter (25 per cent) of the deputies from this linguistic region. In French-speaking Switzerland the proportion of women elected increased but does not exceed 15 per cent of the total number of French-speaking deputies, and that despite the proportion of female candidates (36.6 per cent), which is relatively close to that for German-speaking candidates (35.1 per cent).[16]

If, as a generality, most of the women elected come from left-wing parties, it should also be remembered that a large proportion of the women candidates are presented on the lists of left-wing parties. More-over, the rate of election (i.e. the measure of statistical probability that candidates have of being elected)[17] is generally higher for women who feature on the lists of the Greens, Socialists and Radicals, than for those belonging to other parties. Nonetheless, both the number of female candidates presented by other parties, and their chances of being elected, have increased since 1971.[18]

In general, female candidates receive fewer votes than male candidates, even though an improvement can be detected over the period analysed.

15 Werner Seitz and Madelaine Schneider, *Les femmes et les élections au Conseil National de 1995* (Berne: Office Fédéral de la Statistique, 1995).
16 ibid.
17 The rate of election is calculated by dividing the number of female (or male) candidates elected by the total number of female (or male) candidates, and multiplying by 100.
18 Werner Seitz and Madelaine Schneider, op. cit.

We can see that since 1971 the probability of female candidates being elected was between 2 and 4 times lower than that for male candidates. The proportion of female candidates has more than doubled in the last 25 years, passing from almost one-sixth to over one-third of the total candidatures (from 15.8 per cent to 34.9 per cent).[19] Women candidates, just as with women elected, are distributed unequally according to political orientation. Whilst women were always more visible on the lists of the left-wing and red-green orientated parties, they were also always less well represented on the lists of right-wing parties. Over time, however, the parties have decreased this level of difference, even though it still exists. The need for better female political representation and the increasing presence of women in certain parties has become a political issue that has obliged the other parties to follow suit and conform.

One revealing aspect of the will to feminise the electoral lists is the importance given by the parties to certain criteria. When selecting candidates, political parties should take into account a number of elements. One study shows that in preparing the lists for the elections to the National Council in 1991, the Swiss political parties regarded as priority criteria both regional distribution and the status of the outgoing deputy. The sex of the candidates was only ranked as the third criterion considered in the selection process.[20] Conversely, among the electorate, a survey revealed that in the autumn of 1995 there were fewer women (9.7 per cent) than men (16.5 per cent) who were willing to vote for a female candidate simply because of her sex. The votes for a woman candidate are determined by her competence.This is the view expressed by 81.8 per cent of the women questioned and 71.6 per cent of the men.[21]

Another aspect of the will on the part of the political parties really to feminise the political scene can be detected by analysing the proportion of women among their leading members. In 1991, the female presence varied among the different parties between one-fifth and a quarter of leading members. The majority of left-wing and green parties had

19 ibid.

20 Madelaine Schneider, *Les élections au Conseil National de 1991: Promotion des femmes. Les mesures de promotion en faveur des femmes prises par les partis* (Berne: Office Fédéral de la Statistique, 1995), 35 pp. (p. 13).

21 Béatrice Schaad,'Faut-il à tout prix pousser les femmes en politique? Les Suissesses disent "non"', *Nouveau Quotidien*, 16 octobre 1995, p. 10.

a much higher share of women among their leading members than did the right-wing and 'bourgeois' parties.[22]

The prospect for female candidates to make appearances on television and radio during the electoral campaign presents a good opportunity to become known, even if it is not a determining element in the results. For the elections to the National Council in 1991, a study reveals that such appearances were, at least numerically speaking, equitable for women candidates. The number of appearances made was in proportion to the female presence on the electoral lists (32.2 per cent). Even if, however, there are no major numerical differences within the various media forms,[23] differences can still be detected when a detailed analysis is conducted. For example, the length of interventions made by women candidates is strikingly shorter than that for men candidates.[24] Thus, the opportunities given to women candidates to become known to the public through the media are less significant than those offered to male candidates.

Two of the measures adopted by the parties to encourage the election of women deserve to be mentioned: the presentation of female candidates on separate lists, and quotas in favour of women. The first time a party presented its male and female candidates on separate lists was in the canton of Bern in 1987.[25] Since then this practice has spread. For the elections to the National Council in 1991 a dozen such cases could be found.[26] Again in 1995 women's lists were put forward in several cantons.[27] This measure has not, however, always been favourable to women. Other elements should be taken into consideration when evaluating it. For example, the presence of prestigious male candidates should encourage parties to have a single list combining male and female candidates. Whereas,

22 Madelaine Schneider, op. cit., pp. 20 and 23.
23 ibid., pp. 25–26.
24 Catherine Cossy and Heidi Stutz, 'Emissions électorales: Les candidates jouent les seconds rôles', in *Questions au féminin* (Berne: Commission Fédérale pour les Questions Féminines, 1992), n° 3, pp. 14–36.
25 Thanh-Huyen Ballmer-Cao, 'La représentation des femmes dans les parlements suisses: évolution et perspectives', in Marie-Noël Beauchesne and Lydia Zaïd, eds, *Women's studies. Manuel de ressources* (Brussels: Services Fédéraux des Affaires Scientifiques, Techniques et Culturelles, 1994), pp. 107–117 (p. 113).
26 Madelaine Schneider, op. cit., p. 17, note.
27 Werner Seitz and Madelaine Schneider, op. cit.

on the contrary, when there is a list of male candidates who do not have very high standing, allied to the weakness of a given party, it could be advantageous for female candidates to have separate lists.[28]

The second measure is the system of quotas. This transitional measure, which aims at an equitable representation between men and women in politics, has raised much controversy. In Switzerland, neither parliamentary nor popular initiatives concerning this requirement have had any success. For example, the proposed introduction of a quota system into the legislative institutions of the City of Bern was massively rejected by voters in September 1995. A similar proposition in Luzern had also been rejected a few months before. These outcomes are not surprising if we analyse the opinions of the population on the subject. According to a survey undertaken in October 1995 in French-speaking and German-speaking Switzerland, 65.3 per cent of men and 58.4 per cent of women were not in favour of the introduction of quotas for women candidates.[29] In practice, this opposition exists between parties but also within parties, especially as the federal structure guarantees a lot of independence to its constituent parts. The result is that the system of quotas is very rarely used during the drawing-up of electoral lists. Additionally, the extent to which quotas are adopted or advised varies among the political groupings. It should also be noted that some parties even prefer to avoid the term 'quotas' and use terms such as 'quantified aims' or 'proportional rule', accompanied by simple recommendations.

Let us now examine the female presence in other areas of power. As is the case at the federal level, the average percentage of female representation in the cantonal Parliaments has not ceased growing. Thus, between 1992 and 1994, it averaged 21.3 per cent. Still, the cantonal differences are significant (e.g. from 7.5 per cent in Glaris to 36 per cent in Geneva). The cantons which had introduced political rights for women before 1971 are also those which had better female representation in the cantonal Parliaments. They are also the ones which had a better share of women representatives at the Federal Assembly. Recently, however, this

---

28 See p. 27 in Commission Fédérale pour les Questions Féminines, *Femmes au parlement! Un guide pour les élections fédérales de 1995, à l'intention des partis, des organisations féminines et des médias* (Berne: juin 1994), 53 pp.

29 Béatrice Schaad, op. cit.

phenomenon seems to have decreased, being replaced by an increase in female representation in the cantons that are less 'progressive'.[30] At the local level, the average proportion of women in the communal Legislative Councils has shown an increase to 22.5 per cent by 1990, whereas in the communal Executive Councils it stood at 8.4 per cent in 1988.[31]

Progressively, women have also held or currently hold seats in several cantonal Executive Councils. In April 1994, the canton of Bern was the first in Switzerland to have two women councillors. It was followed by Appenzell Outer Rhodes, the penultimate canton to accord women their political rights! Some time later, the city of Bern was the first to have an Executive Council composed mainly of women. On the Federal Executive Council, Ruth Dreifuss is the only woman to have held a seat, since 1993, among the seven members. Before her, another woman, Elisabeth Kopp, had held a seat. Progressively, then, women are occupying posts of high responsibility. The presidency of the National Council, for example, has already been occupied by three women.

Some inferences can be drawn by way of conclusion. It could be asserted that female presence in the political institutions of Switzerland is increasing continuously, even though inequality still exists. Of course, whether in Switzerland or in other countries, equality of political representation is still far from being fully achieved, though examples prove that it is possible. We can actually see such examples when Green and 'alternative' political groupings present and elect a majority of women. It has also been seen in the majority female composition of the Executive Council of the City of Bern. It is true that such cases are sporadic, but they exist in a country which, only 25 years ago, legally prohibited the political equality of women. This implies that, within a few decades, Swiss women have been able to integrate relatively well into

30 Thanh-Huyen Ballmer-Cao and John Bendix, 'La représentation des femmes au Conseil National: Analyse de quelques déterminants et possibilités de promotion', in *La difficile conquête du mandat de députée. Les femmes et les élections au Conseil National de 1971 à 1991* (Berne: Office Fédéral de la Statistique, 1994), pp. 125–139.
31 Claire Jobin et al., in *Vers l'égalité. Aperçu statistique de la situation des femmes et des hommes en Suisse* (Berne: Office Fédéral de la Statistique, 1994), 138 pp. (pp. 132–133).

the political sphere. Even if Switzerland is still not on the same level as the Nordic countries in terms of political equality, it is certainly positioned within a good European average. Of course, this affirmation should be considered with due relativity to the spheres and periods analysed. If we look back to the past, and more precisely to the year 1971, we can confirm that a lot of progress has been made, and that quite probably this progress has been achieved rather more quickly than would have been expected considering the lateness of the entry of women into the political arena. In parallel to this, it is still difficult to justify the continuing lack of equality on a practical level since the time of the formal introduction of the principle of political equality. It is true that, considered from this point of view, and as we look ahead towards the future, the progress made thus far does not even seem to represent half the path along which women should proceed before they see the principle of political equality fully applied. This is the very principle which was formally recognised 25 years ago.

Annelies Debrunner

Women in Public Office in Switzerland

My remarks on 'Women in Public Office' are based, at a theoretical level, on specialist literature, statistics and interviews with those responsible for ensuring equality and with women in public office. At the practical, everyday level, I have my own experience, especially in the last five years as the person responsible for cultural matters in Weinfelden, a small town near Lake Constance in Northeastern Switzerland. From the end of the 1960s onwards, I was also for many years a primary school teacher.

My paper is divided into four parts: firstly, the specific Swiss situation; secondly, women in government administration; thirdly, the offices for equal opportunities and women's issues; and fourthly, a short concluding note. In this huge topic 'Women in Public Office', I will be dealing in particular with the structural and cultural background to women working in public administration.

1. The Specific Swiss Situation

Administrations, as concerns of the state, vary from country to country in terms of size, density and outlook of the population, number of languages, financial resources, system of government (degree of democracy, federalism or centralisation etc.). In the Swiss system of government, the federal principle is very clearly defined in relation to public administrations. In many areas of administration, there is autonomy down as far as the smallest unit. No rules can be set forth for this, rather it is the exception which is the rule. Thus there exists at the level of community, canton and nation an executive, usually a legislative (in small communities this is all the male and female citizens), and an administration. There is judicial power at national, cantonal and district level. And, depending on the area of administration, there is legislative autonomy at the level of community, district, canton and state. For example, each of the 26 cantons has its own legislation on building, on provision of care, on culture etc. Cantonal agreements then regulate this multiplicity at points of overlap.

I should like specially to mention education. Laws on teaching, laws about schools and the way these laws are applied, curricula – all these are matters for the cantons. On the other hand, the communities are responsible for the school buildings and for the appointment of teachers. The management of kindergartens is in most cantons within the sphere of competence of the communities. With the exception of the Federal Technical Universities in Zürich and Lausanne, all universities, institutes of higher education and senior secondary schools are cantonal places of education.

Today, especially with previously unknown possibilities for mobility, the federal principle is often looked upon as a hindrance. If we look at administration, administrations at all three levels are very autonomous in individual areas. Important prerequisites for administrative efficiency in such a complicated national set-up are a tight structure, a clearly defined hierarchy and the observance of procedures wherever possible.

As regards the specific Swiss situation, I have given you a short overview of our system of government. I now turn to the matter of equality. Swiss women have been eligible to vote and to stand for office for 25 years, therefore they came of age politically in 1971. The new marriage law of 1986 and the equal opportunities article of 1981 have further secured the possibilities of equality within Swiss law. Soon the law guaranteeing equal legal status to men and women will come into effect.[1] In some cantons, it had already been possible for women to participate in decision-making at a political, educational or church level. For example, it was possible for the women of Neuchâtel to be elected to school boards from 1908.[2]

At the level of administration and in political offices, there are – with such complicated structures – many small jobs which can be carried out in an honorary capacity or by a small part-time appointment. This also

1 Susanne Woodtli, *Gleichberechtigung* (Frauenfeld: Huber, 1983).
2 Lotti Ruckstuhl, *Frauen sprengen Fesseln. Hindernislauf zum Frauenstimmrecht in der Schweiz* (Bonstetten: Interfeminas, n.d.), p. 150.
   François Höpflinger, Maria Charles, Annelies Debrunner, *Familienleben und Berufsarbeit. Zum Wechselverhältnis zweier Lebensbereiche* (Zürich: Seismo, 1991).

often makes it possible for women to get into an area of public administration, to take up their first duties in the public domain. Particularly
for Swiss women, this is an opportunity to be able to combine work
for the community at large with family obligations. In Switzerland, the
19th century *bourgeois* ideal of the family still influences cultural patterns
today. In general terms, even today the normal biography of a woman
in Switzerland is characterised by marriage and motherhood. And it is
very much part of the norm that women adjust their lives to those of
their partners and those dear to them.[3]

The classic role model – housewife and provider – is still frequently
to be met, but is in decline. In 1980, the proportion of families with
father in full employment and mother not in employment was 64 per
cent, in 1990 this had gone down to 51 per cent. Women with small
children are still rarely in full employment: in 1980 9.4 per cent, in 1990
10.8 per cent. (These are mothers in households with couples whose
youngest child is less than one year old).[4] On the other hand, the proportion of women with children who are in part-time employment has
risen. In 1980, this was 20.3 per cent, rising in 1990 to 31 per cent.
Every fifth person in Switzerland (19.8 per cent) is in part-time employment, and part-time employment is largely a matter for women; 80
per cent of those in part-time employment are women.[5] In addition,
the Swiss education system has no all-day schools. It is only in recent
times that efforts in this direction have been made in progressive cities
and areas. Moreover, school hours and holidays vary a lot. Thus individual care by someone to whom the child can relate – usually the
mother – is an important task. In addition, the educational norms and
the disadvantageous environment for children at the end of the twentieth century also make individual care necessary. Yet in the last decades

---

3 Anna Borkowsky, Katharina Ley, Ursula Streckeisen, *Strukturelle und subjektive*
   Aspekte von Arbeitsbiographen, Erwerbsverläufen und Berufslaufbahnen von Frauen
   (Schlussbericht an den Schweizerischen Nationalfonds, Bern, 1985).
   Annelies Debrunner, *Gelebte Wirklichkeit – erträumte Zukunft. Gespräche mit Frauen*
   des Jahrgangs 57 (Zürich: Seismo, 1996).
4 Bundesamt für Statistik, *Familien heute. Das Bild der Familie in der Volkzählung*
   1990 (Bern: EDMZ, 1994), p. 81.
5 Bundesamt für Statistik, *Auf dem Weg zur Gleichstellung? Frauen und Männer in*
   der Schweiz aus statistischer Sicht (Bern: EDMZ, 1993), p. 51.

the proportion of women amongst those in employment has increased. After remaining stable until the end of the 1960s at about a third, it rose steadily from 1970 (33.8 per cent) and reached 38 per cent in 1990. However, only 47.6 per cent of women in employment work full-time.[6]

2. *Women in Public Administration*

Behind the fact that equality for women in the public domain is so new, there are norms, values, structures and historical contexts. Until the end of the 19th century, the office was in general an exclusively male domain. All written work was carried out until then by a clerk.[7] It was not until the advent of shorthand, the telephone and the typewriter in offices that female office employees were appointed to carry out the clerical work. They had possibilities of employment particularly because male clerks often 'refused for reasons of professional and social pride ... to use the typewriters and to take shorthand notes to dictation'.[8]

Thus entry for women to positions in public service became easier. In the Federal Administration, the first typewriter appeared in 1885. Soon the first women typist took up her position. The '*Fräuleins*', as they were called, were particularly adept with the new machines so that men willingly entrusted them to women. Already by 1900 in the service sector in Switzerland, 12 per cent of the employees were women. The 'female assistants' usually had no training. Until the beginning of the 20th century, the Swiss Clerks Association refused to accept women into its training courses.[9] It is also worth mentioning that into the last third of our century there existed in places laws governing civil servants which laid down that the wife of a civil servant could not stand for elected office.

6 Bundesamt für Statistik, *Auf dem Weg zur Gleichstellung? Frauen und Männer in der Schweiz aus statistischer Sicht* (Bern: EDMZ, 1993).
7 Eidgenössische Kommission für Frauenfragen, *Auswirkungen neuer Techniken auf Frauenarbeitsplätze im Büro- und Verwaltungsbereich* (Bern: EDMZ, 1988), p. 17.
8 Elisabeth Joris, Heidi Witzig, *Frauengeschichte(n) Dokumente aus zwei Jahrhunderten zur Situation der Frau in der Schweiz* (Zürich: Limmat, 1986), p. 199.
9 Joris and Witzig, p. 199.

Senior management or typist? Where are women today, at the end of the 20th century, in public service? We are especially interested in the first possibility. Certainly there must be a correspondence between individual wishes and possibilities if women want to make careers at all. In general terms, a woman asks herself the question far more than a man does: how can I best combine a strong commitment to my profession with family commitments? Or do I go for – in our case – professional work, a career?

So it is no surprise that on the basis of this social situation, of current values and of present-day structures that even at the end of the 20th century very few women are top civil servants. In general terms, male and female civil servants are to be found in the top echelon of the hierarchical structure. Increasing confinement of civil servants to the highest echelons of the hierarchy, which has been noted in recent years, as a consequence affects women very severely. For just as in business, in the field of education and higher education, women are rarely to be found in top administrative positions. Three per cent are female.

However, it is particularly in Switzerland that a female elite has succeeded in advancing into male domains. If we compare the figures for 1970 and 1990, the proportion of women doctors has risen from 13.9 per cent to 23 per cent.[10] But figures are unfortunately not available for the proportion of women civil servants. However, we do know that the proportion of women in more skilled professions in federal government has risen from 5.7 per cent to 12.9 per cent.

What are the particular conditions of work in government administrations? In government administrations, there is often a less flexible framework structure. As I mentioned at the outset, this is determined by the interconnections of the political system. Additionally, it is less usual than in the private sector to find the dynamic, flexible, innovative colleague.[11] However, administrations tend to be a protected area. They are less exposed to economic factors which sometimes change

10 Maria Charles, *Berufliche Gleichstellung – ein Mythos? Geschlechter-Segregation in der schweizerischen Berufswelt* (Bern: EDMZ, 1995).
11 Eidgenössisches Büro für die Gleichstellung von Frau und Mann, *Betriebliche Gleichstellung von Frau und Mann. Erfahrungen aus vier Unternehmen* (Bern: EDMZ, 1993).

rapidly. A portion of the employees in administrations, especially those in higher positions, have the status of civil servants and are thus nominated by the executive for a period of office of four years.

To bring about change, initiatives certainly have to be started on various levels. In what follows, I am going to present you with a list of conditions which have to be met as fully as possible to smooth the path of a woman into a management job in an administration.

Ideal Conditions for a Woman Wanting a Career

Structural level:
- A boss of the new generation (personality takes precedence over sex)
- short distance to work
- being in the right place at the right time to seize the right opportunity
- in general, active support for women, i.e. mentoring, advice, protected area

Individual level:
A woman, in addition to her skills, brings the following qualities:
- drive, 'cheekiness'
- above-average training
- ability to delegate private 'problems' and tasks
- tendency to be pragmatic
- high acceptance of existing structures
- ability to adapt to structures
- patience
- enjoyment of a heavy work-load
- ability to plan her own future

If there is a discrepancy between the ideal and reality, the personal initiative, the energy and the creativity of women are all the more in demand to produce unconventional solutions. A senior woman civil servant remarked on these points: 'I've often had to fight to maintain my position so that I could accept responsibility and not be treated as a helpless creature'. An important source of support in the process of equality are often the offices for women's issues.

3. Offices for Women's Issues / for Equality

In Switzerland, too, there are at national level and in some cantons and cities, offices for women's issues. Their aim is to help towards the achievement of equality for women. Some offices exist specifically for women in administrations. At federal level, the Staff Office for Women's Issues has been in existence since 1981.[12] Its remit relates to internal administrative matters and it supports the improvement of the position of women in the administration. In particular, the advance of women into the higher salary brackets is to be encouraged, part-time work is to be maximised in all areas, training, in-service courses and career planning are to be improved. The use of non-sexist language is an area supported by active policies for equality. The general aim is to ensure that the rights and directives enshrined in law are translated into practice. For example, in Zürich, where there has been a Staff Office for Women's Issues since 1987, the participation of the director of the Office in recasting the regulations regarding personnel was an important element of her work. The most important regulations governing the active promotion of women and their equality are contained in this:

- taking into account non-professional experience when the starting salary is determined
- re-training for former male and female employees, advice on how to resume one's career
- 16 weeks paid maternity leave with paid time off for breast-feeding (1/4 of normal working hours up to a maximum of 1 year)
- right to paid leave for parental and family commitments (up to 3 days per occasion)
- looking after dependents (from the age of 2), right to an additional week of annual leave
- right to leave on half-pay for women employees with children whose husbands are doing military service or civil defence work
- five days paid leave for fathers at the birth of a child and the possibility of three weeks unpaid leave during the first two years of the child's life

12 Federal Commission of Women's Issues (Ed), *Great Achievements – Small Changes? On the Situation of Women in Switzerland* (Bern: EDMZ, 1995), p. 36.

- equality of part-time employees and eligibility to stand for elected office if doing at least a 50 per cent work-load
- creation of working conditions which eliminate sexual harassment and discrimination of all kinds; right of the Office for Women's Issues to start disciplinary proceedings
- equal linguistic treatment of men and women.

So the normal work of those responsible for women's issues consists of collaborating on the establishment of rules and regulations to do with personnel matters, of disseminating information and in general raising the level of awareness, especially of those in leading positions. Individual consultations with women are also important.

Of course, at a time of crisis the question arises repeatedly as to whether there is a justification for jobs which do not pay for themselves in terms of hard, market-orientated considerations – but which, in soft, longer-term, market-orientated considerations, do in fact have the ability to yield important values.

4. Concluding Note

On the one hand, it is true that women in Switzerland do not have a tradition of operating in public office. On the other hand, we have for that reason for decades looked after niches. These consisted of working for public charities. There is a long tradition of work in institutions for the public good. We also know that a female elite has grown bigger – I mentioned women doctors, women in the legal profession and in higher professions in the Federation. My Utopia envisages that we bring to public life an increase in basic qualities of caring and human concern linked to entrepreneurial ability and drive, which are traditionally male qualities.

(Translated by Malcolm Pender)

Various facts and dates were kindly provided by the following organisations:
Eidgenössisches Personalamt, Stabsstelle für Frauenfragen, Bern; Fachstelle für Frauenfragen der Stadt Zürich; Fachstelle für Gleichberechtigungsfragen Stadt Winterthur; Frauenbeauftragte Stadt Konstanz (Germany).

YVETTE JAGGI

Swiss Women's Long March to Equality

I would like to discuss Swiss women's long march to equality from two angles. Firstly, in law, on the federal or cantonal level, and secondly in life, particularly in professional and everyday life. A very long march, indeed, but not at all a desperate one; for each sign of progress, even the smallest one, gives courage to go further. And you know the deep motivation, the secret of all people who are struggling for a just cause and thus working for the future: yesterday's utopia has become today's reality, what seems improbable today will be self-evident tomorrow.

In comparison to the bicentennial of this University, celebrated with the beautiful slogan, '200 Years of Useful Learning' winning woman's rights seems to be a very recent movement in Switzerland. Women in Switzerland have only had the right to vote at the Federal level since 1971 – a state of affairs which had previously given rise to situations verging on the ridiculous, such as when the Mayor of Geneva, Lise Girardin, did not have the right to express her opinion on subjects of national importance. Twenty-five years is a short period, even if the right to vote now seems self-evident to many. Having come to politics late, Swiss women have worked double time to make up for the late start, increasing their numbers with each election for the Federal Parliament. And, in March 1993, thanks to an extraordinary mobilisation of women all over the country and in Bern, the federal capital, they even imposed one of their own in the Federal Council, the government of the Swiss Confederation.

Their presence in the political arena, in quality more than quantity, should not obscure the fact that they are more often than not absent from the economic arena, where, precisely, decisions are taken, where real power is concentrated and shared – between male insiders of course. Thus, having progressively taken their position within the political institutions, women should move to take their place in the economic strongholds.

Equality of Civic Rights and Women's Place in Politics

Women made a late entry into political life in Switzerland, but in rapidly increasing numbers. This evolution will no doubt be confirmed particularly if economic power increasingly predominates over political power. Women can at least be satisfied with the latter.

The Right to Vote and to Hold Office
Switzerland's prolonged delay in the field of civic rights has prompted a great deal of irony. Yet, women's right to vote and to hold office had to be the subject of a national ballot and had to win both a popular and cantonal majority. The first ballot, in February 1959, failed at the federal level. I am proud to say that it was a success in my canton, which had the good idea of coupling two votes, one on the Confederation level, the other on the Canton of Vaud level.

Within the legislative framework, as women's suffrage was extended to the different levels, women stood for election to the Federal Parliament as of autumn 1971 and to the cantonal parliaments as soon as was possible. Contrary to what was experienced abroad, where the number of women in parliament remained a near constant (most notably in the UK and the USA), or regressed (in France), the number of women elected to the National Council (Lower House) kept increasing from one election to the next: 10 women elected out of 200 seats in 1971, 15 in 1975, 21 in 1979, 22 in 1983, 29 in 1987, 35 in 1991, and 43 in 1995 (42 women took the oath of office, as Vreni Spoerri was elected to the Upper House). In twenty-five years, the proportion of women elected to the National Council went from 5 per cent to 21.5 per cent, a progression and achievement indeed honourable when compared to results internationally. However, these scores are relative: out of 990 candidates 43 women elected represent 4.3 per cent, whereas for men, out of 1944 candidates, 157 elected represent 8.5 per cent. In other words: women have one chance in 25.5 of being elected, men one in 11.7. In the cantonal parliaments, the proportion of women has on average doubled in ten years, going from 10 to 20 per cent between 1983 and 1993. At present, women represent 7 to 35 per cent of those elected, depending on the canton. The record is held by Geneva.

In order to appreciate fully the electoral success of women in the parliamentary assemblies, you have to realise that their members are elected through a proportional list system (seats attributed in proportion to the party list voted for), and serve according to a militia system, earning indemnities which are fairly low and thus require those holding office to maintain their professional activity, at least on a part-time basis. For elections decided by an absolute majority (usually requiring two ballots), election is obviously more expensive, full-time positions still rare, remuneration in general more substantial, and women elected – therefore – in noticeably smaller numbers. Abetted by the electorate's conservative reflex, men do not easily give up their seat to women newcomers to politics; they feel distrustful about these women who often declare and adopt a non-conformist attitude. It is to be noted that the lobbies, too, do not much appreciate 'these ladies', most of whom take the luxury of not tying themselves to interest groups, obstinately preferring to exercise their mandate independently. Note that their own political parties complain as well. Generally speaking, and independent of either the method or the level of the ballot, the left-wing voter and the ecologist tend to favour female candidates, while the right-wing voter, particularly of the agrarian party, still manifests a traditional preference for male politics.

In the States Council (the Upper House where each canton is represented by two deputies), the number of women has varied from 1 to 8 (out of 46), which represents between 2.2 per cent and 17.4 per cent. Note that since 1995, for two cantons, Zurich and Geneva, both deputies are women. When considering the women elected to political office, the executive branch should not be forgotten. In the cantonal governments, the proportion of women has risen to approximately 10 per cent of those elected. In the executive branch of the country's major cities, the proportion of women easily exceeds ten percent, the city of Bern distinguishing itself with a municipal government composed of four women and three men (of which the president).

At the highest level, the Federal Council, the collegiate body of seven members, exercises executive power in Switzerland. Elected by the 246 members of the Federal Parliament, the 'Seven Wise Men' formed an exclusively masculine circle for many years. In 1983, the Socialist party proposed the candidacy of a woman, Lilian Uchtenhagen, to the Federal

Council to succeed one of their recently deceased members. A male Socialist, Otto Stich, was given preference. But ten months later, when
choosing the successor to a resigning Radical party member, the Federal
Parliament elected another National Councillor from Zurich, a woman
named Elisabeth Kopp. Weakened by the shaky professional affairs of her
husband, she had to submit her resignation in January 1989.

This untimely episode with Elisabeth Kopp might seem to have post-
poned any idea of a female candidacy to the Federal Council for a long
time. In fact, four years elapsed before the Socialists again had the opportunity of presenting one of their own. They nominated the National
Councillor Christiane Brunner but the Houses of Parliament again
preferred a man, Francis Matthey – who had the strength of character
to refuse his election, opening the way to the union secretary, Ruth
Dreifuss. She thus became the hundredth member – and second woman
– of the Federal Council on March 10th, 1993 and must answer to extremely high expectations, particularly on the part of those women who
were actively mobilised for a woman who could represent and defend
them at the highest level of power in Switzerland.

Obviously, the presence of only one woman in the Federal Council, even one as excellent as Ruth Dreifuss, cannot entirely eliminate
the notion of token representation, just enough to stroke the good conscience of some and not too many to provoke the ill humour of others. From this was born the idea of a nation-wide, popular initiative 'For
an equitable representation of women in the federal government'. In
1994, a committee collected over 100,000 signatures of citizens prepared
to support the principle of power-sharing between men and women at
every level of the Federal government and Parliament being written into
the Federal Constitution. This claim, which only recently would have
prompted smirks or rage, now appears acceptable to many people in
Switzerland. However, the project of a new Federal Constitution, which
is now under discussion, simply ignores this claim.

Now a small recapitulation of some of today's victories and tomorrow's
battles. From an institutional point of view, a number of observations
encourage optimism:

Swiss women, despite the particular requirements of a semi-direct democracy with the aforementioned requirement of a double majority,

have become citizens in their own right, with equal rights according to Article 4 of the Federal Constitution, revised in 1971 (civic rights) and in 1981 (civil rights).

Committees of equality are working at the federal level (administration and public corporations) as well as at cantonal and municipal levels to pursue the long march towards equality, in the absence of a 'Minister of Women's Affairs', unthinkable in a country as federalist as Switzerland.

Laws, regulations and other official documents are written in gender-neutral terms, their authors having received specific guidelines on the terminology to be used – vocabulary is never completely innocent – in accordance with the new, legal situation.

The conditions have been put in place that promote absolute equality for women, and thus, their access to those powers that men have too long reserved exclusively for themselves. In order to break this monopoly, tied to a traditional division of labour in our western civilisation, it will take more than even the most inspired intervention on the part of the legislator.

Thus, another series of observations encourage a more shaded appreciation of progress in the strictly formal domain of legislation. Firstly, it is not enough to accede to a position of power in order to exercise it fully:

either, it is abandoned for subjective reasons: women, who represent an important part of the electorate, give up their majority power in so far as they vote along other than strictly sexual lines. Likewise, women promoted to positions of management do not always exercise the stubbornness required to dominate, invoking other priorities, most notably personal and family,
or, it is lost for external reasons: power seems to escape from positions in proportion to women's investiture of them. Thus, as the influence of parliamentary assemblies declines in favour of technostructures, it appears strange to witness women taking their place in numbers in the former and yet remaining so outnumbered at the higher levels of management. Likewise, women do not sufficiently assert their presence in the technical fields, such as planning and urban development; they fail to make the most of their knowledge and experience.

In order to accelerate the advancement of women, provoking them if necessary, one solution can be envisaged: the introduction of quotas. Hotly debated, particularly in German-speaking Switzerland, where two negative votes have been registered in Bern and Lucerne, the quota system is attractive, but only as a temporary measure. Because quantifiable objectives would be established, the degree of success could be measured: so many women elected, promoted, etc. within a certain time-period, also fixed in advance. Depending upon the givens when fixing the quota to be attained, it must be sufficiently high to be challenging, but not so high as to be discouraging. Decidedly, the entire philosophical debate of a quota system and the opportunity of enacting some variant will dominate discussion in Switzerland in the coming years.

Equality of Civil Rights and the March towards Equality of Opportunity

Without any doubt, the women's cause has advanced more during the last 20 to 25 years than during the entire history of the country. The progress can be measured by rereading the vast *Report on the Position of Women in Switzerland*, published in several volumes by the Federal Commission for the Question of Women during the years 1979–1984. In fact, the introduction and generalisation of women's right to vote and to hold office at all levels of Swiss democratic institutions, as well as the promotion of equality between men and women in the family, at school and at work, have been made possible during the last two decades. Whereas the slow conquest of judicial equality continues, the struggle has henceforth begun to acquire the elusive equality of opportunity, in professional life to begin with.

Article 4 of the Constitution

Once civic equality was recognised, Swiss women quickly understood that other discriminations from which they suffered ought to be eliminated. They also rapidly understood that the long and laborious route towards the numerous revisions of the law that must be foreseen could not be undertaken without a solid and unquestionable constitutional basis. Thus, a national, popular initiative for equality of rights in the family, at school and in the workplace was launched at the end of 1975, proclaimed Year of the Woman by the UN. Subsequently, this initiative was withdrawn in favour of a counter-project, formulated (better) by the Federal parliament and accepted by popular vote – a comfortable double majority of both the people and the cantons – on 14 June 1981. This date, rightly considered historic by Swiss women, gave rise to a nationwide, women's strike – also considered historic – in 1991, despite differences in turnout in the cities and the countryside.

The consequences of the new Constitutional Article 4, al. 2, are such that the Federal Council, at the request moreover of Parliament, had to set up a legislative programme to eliminate discriminatory provisions in Swiss law. Implementing this programme, which requires revising all the laws wherein men and women are not treated equally, may well not be completed before the end of this century. Of course, since 1981 no further discriminatory laws have been introduced.

Without enumerating the numerous rules necessitating review, it can be observed that the resistance is strongest, the technically-motivated objections (concerning enforcement) the most vigorous, and thus the alibis most cleverly elaborated when it comes to eliminating discrimination where women pay the price, in the strictest sense of the word. To put it bluntly, the battle for equal rights becomes particularly rough the moment economic interests come into play.

Generally speaking, the lawmaker gives absolutely nothing away to women, neither in family rights, nor in public education, nor in social insurance, and even less in the workplace where equal treatment has a price, usually to the employer. The latter obviously puts his economic interest above that which is, in our eyes, an imperative of social justice.

The Law concerning Equality of Men and Women
In order to avoid the long detour of ad hoc legislation, the constituent took the precaution of affirming the particular characteristic of the rule relating to 'an equal salary for work of equal value', a rule that can be invoked before a judge by any person convinced of discrimination at the salary level. Concerning direct enforcement, the few instances where action was taken gave rise to difficult and involved procedures with inconclusive results. Beyond the hazardous nature of all judicial procedures, these cases showed that, in practice and to all intents and purposes,

the constitutional clause would be a dead letter, unless legislation specifying its application was passed – precisely the legislation that was to be avoided.

So, after about ten years of discussions and equivocations, reports and counter-evaluations, projects and consultations, the Federal Council ended up by submitting a law on 24 February 1993, for equality between men and women (rebaptised by the National Council the law for equality between women and men). The text, adopted by both houses of Parliament on 24 March 1995 will become law on July 1st 1996. It concerns, essentially, the right to equal remuneration and provides the means for its application, notably by inverting the burden of proof, and by giving female employees the possibility of lodging a complaint, of being assisted by a union organisation, and by prohibiting all measures of pressure against them on the part of the employer, etc.

The law coming into force will bring great improvements, but no doubt for many years to come, women will continue to be discriminated against at the collocation level on the scale applied to the civil service where equal pay within each class has long since been enacted. Just as in those countries where some form of Equal Pay Act has existed for two or three decades, Swiss women will also have to bide time before being able to eliminate salary discrimination in the private sector of the economy.

According to official surveys on salaries in industry and trade, the average difference between men and women remains at about 33 per cent. Even if the level of education – often lower for women – and the relatively shorter and disrupted professional 'career' is taken into account, women in the private sector remain victims of a 'net' discrimination of over 15 per cent. Which is strictly unacceptable in a country such as Switzerland where pride in the state of law is taken very seriously and where nothing is more detestable than pompous or partially applicable texts.

Women and the Workplace
Equality of pay is far from the norm, the new law recognising the respect of only certain rights and only if it is applied. Furthermore, there is a very real risk given the economic situation that we are witnessing today: that of women's exclusion from the higher spheres of the economy. During

the eighties, the service sector (banks and insurance) seemed more than willing to welcome women, but not in all types of services, for those with high added-value were reserved for men. Now, the following question has to be asked: in periods of economic down-turn, are women not purely and simply, almost naturally, excluded from the work-place, no matter the economic sector, service or secondary? Are there, among the high-level employees of industrial or commercial companies, women who were not appointed to a management position for exclusively family reasons (inheritance, marriage, etc.)?

To answer these questions amounts to alluding to a – small – group of special cases, so rare are the women who belong either to a directorial team, or the board of directors of companies based in Switzerland. With a kind of complacency tinged with quite a bad conscience, the specialised press periodically takes an inventory of women in management. There are, at present, undoubtedly fewer than one hundred out of several thousand upper-level managers in the 500 largest companies in the country. On average, the proportion barely exceeds 1 per cent, except of course in the three traditionally 'female' sectors: the hotel sector, an important economic branch in Switzerland, the personal care sector, and the medico-social sector.

And yet, women already represent 15–20 per cent of the students of economics in Swiss universities and make up at least one-tenth of the graduate business school candidates for an MBA. It is clear that even with their higher rate of success in the final exams and armed with the same degree, women do not follow the same career path as their male colleagues. In reality, and despite a higher 'drop-out' rate of women earning a degree, there is a real inequality of opportunity throughout a woman's professional life.

Like discrimination at the salary level, unequal opportunity is the result of well-known circumstances: women often follow a discontinuous career, with an interruption while their children are young, or a temporarily reduced working week, for example. But these exceptions do not explain everything; instinctively, bosses will still often hesitate to confer responsibilities on women, who have a – false – reputation of higher absenteeism than men, and are – rightly – less career-driven than them, that is to say less readily prepared to sacrifice the quality of their personal and family life in order to scale the professional ladder. In short, because

women show less hunger for power within a company, they merit less
to receive this same power that men are only too happy to reserve and
exercise exclusively by themselves, according to the 'good old tradition'.

To counter this spontaneous imbalance, it is necessary to fall back on
positive measures, which make up the wide palette of interventions both
enacted and in preparation, in order to improve the basic conditions for
the promotion of equality between women and men. A vast programme,
in fact, requiring the participation of all the progressive forces of society for its fulfillment. And it can be fulfilled, because of the diversity
of positive measures, also called incentives: from the creation of a company nursery to the stated preference for women candidates for a particular position, to courses in confidence-building, exercises in self-de-
fence or the possibility of back-to-work programmes after several years
of career interruption. The numerous and diversified initiatives taken
in Switzerland these last years, with of course unequal yet encouraging success, will continue to multiply.

Equality of Opportunity in Everyday Life

Equality in everyday life is more than the consequence of the civic and
civil rights we have been discussing. It is a matter of changing mentalities, attitudes and behaviour. This profound reform must take place in
the hearts and minds and – most difficult of all – on a daily basis. Not
in words, but in deeds. Not in theory, but in practice. The gulf that in
general separates the speech which can be proclaimed and the reality
which must be lived is well-known. Let me quote three examples relative to public and private life:

women and the city
women and activity in the defence of the consumer
women and men: division of household tasks

Women and the City
The task of the planning and development of urban agglomerations
is one in which women have an important role to play in the coming

years. Today, in Switzerland, more than two-thirds of the population live in an urban agglomeration. The city is a territory, a domain where women must invest their talent. Their relation to space would seem to be strongly influenced by their roles in biological reproduction and in the social unit of the family. Yet they remain essentially users of the public domain and consumers of private dwellings, both having been planned and developed by men.

On the occasion of the OECD's international conference, 'Women and the City: Housing, Services and Urban Environment' held in Paris in October 1994, it became apparent that there is a necessity for active women (professionally or within group associations, for example) to become involved in all the issues relating to the framework of urban life, and to force the authorities to take notice of their opinions. Elected women for their part must take responsibility for recognising these needs, and take adequate measures favouring the quality of urban life for women, and through them, for the population as a whole.

For many women throughout the world and also in Switzerland, the city has become synonymous with violence. It would be vain to deny the risk inherent in city life. But it would be equally wrong to deny that cities are also a place of emancipation and awakening because of the education, training, varied job opportunities and cultural activities they offer. These roles of the city are to be encouraged because women benefit from them.

In planning and urban development, infrastructure and equipment remain the domain of male technicians and yet women have needs, notably commodities and security, to put forward, the provision of which depends less on technical or aesthetic prowess, and more on a practical sense and awareness of the needs of others. Female specialists must come forward and make known their reflections and suggestions in order that the preoccupations of daily life be taken into account with the same degree of seriousness as the so-called 'necessities' and other technical constraints.

In the field of durable planning and development, in urban regions in particular, our general well-being dictates a greater contribution on the part of women, more sensitive to social preoccupations in the long-term – for a generation in any event. The future of cities and the quality of life that can be led there will be favourably influenced.

In Defence of the Consumer

If there is a movement in which women straightaway took the lead – and lead it still – it is the consumer movement. Women have made it their business to defend and inform consumers in Switzerland since the movement's beginning about thirty years ago. It would be difficult to find this exclusivity elsewhere, except perhaps in Japan where the house-wives' league has a certain tradition.

Since their beginning, the leading consumer organisations, which have often reconfirmed their desire to remain women's organisations, have proven to be an effective economic and social training ground. It is in analysing the goods and services proliferating in the marketplace that women have learned the essential mechanisms of national and in-ternational economics, as well as the characteristics of the society of mass consumption in which we live today – this, in spite of the gener-alised recession and increasing under-employment in the industrialised countries. A training ground for information, information that is ac-quired and must be appraised with a healthy suspicion, and informa-tion that is diffused, free of errors and approximations likely to mar the credibility of consumers' arguments, essential to all consumer defence organisations. Further, this type of organisation is an excellent on-the-job training ground in management skills. Even in a country as small as Switzerland, the consumer defence organisations have taken on im-portant dimensions. Witness the largest – and the oldest, founded in 1959 – the French-Swiss Association of Consumers (FRC) that I had the honour of running from 1973 to 1979, a genuine firm with a turno-ver of two and a half million Swiss francs – not exactly a rest cure.

In time, the FRC, and the other early, more or less structured, asso-ciations became real pressure groups, with a staff of professionals capa-ble of effective intervention. And so it was that the consumer associations were able to propose and influence the favourable vote, first by the Houses of Parliament and then by a double majority of the population and can-tons, for a popular initiative leading to the inscription in the Federal Con-stitution of a permanent surveillance of the cost of goods and services, both public and private. A rare exploit in the history of Swiss politics – in 1982 – and the first time this had succeeded since the end of the war.

The previous year, the consumers' groups had already seen their ef-forts rewarded, their aim being the recognition of the consumers' role in the economy and society through a specific line in the basic Charter. This was accepted by popular vote on 14 June 1981, an historic date for Swiss democracy, because on the same day, by a popular and cantonal majority, two new articles were written into the Constitution: the first, accepting the principle of equal rights for men and women and the second, recognising the right of consumers to protection and of their associations to a modest contribution from the Confederation.

It is to be noted that the consumers' associations were revealed not only to be excellent training grounds for citizens and consumers, but also trampolines for election to political office in cantonal parliaments, in Federal Parliament, even in the local executive branch. I am an example, like other former members of associations, in the German-speaking and Italian-speaking parts of Switzerland where the rules of incompatibility are less strictly enforced than in the French-speaking part.

The Division of Household Tasks
The idea of quite another division of household tasks, which has fallen traditionally to women, has made great headway. Thus, the 'new fathers', who are willing to take a role in the education of their children, going beyond simple play. Man has felt boosted by his new task and he is ready to give of himself, with as a bonus a certain pleasure. However, as yet, the household remains a woman's task. In order that sharing become a natural reflex at this level, the education of little girls and, even more important, of little boys is crucial.

This necessity is reinforced by the growing multi-cultural character of our society, through the arrival of people with cultures totally different from our own. It is so true that even today, it is difficult for certain men to admit they are not, or are no longer, the 'boss' of the family they once were. Especially if they have a profession in which they are not made to feel important. The process of behavioural adaptation, by its nature, is exceedingly slow, and frustrates more than one; this to the point where some women have the impression that reforms and social advancement of interest mainly to women take longer to be accepted than other reforms. One evident illustration is the very long battle to obtain in Switzerland (where 26 education systems exist!) what is tradition in Great Britain: the all-day school, so useful for professional mothers and their children.

Important steps have been taken, but the present situation remains fragile. During the next twenty-five years – and perhaps even more – women will face many struggles in their quest for a more equitable sharing of responsibilities and power in collaboration with emancipated men, for it is self-evident that the advancement of women can only be accomplished in tandem with the liberation of men.

My concluding message is quite simple: like men, but in their own subtle and pragmatic way, women have to be wherever power is. First of all on the political scene of course. But more and more in the social and business world, on the higher level in big and smaller firms, in professional associations, in education institutions, in trade unions, in 'new' movements and pressure groups: consumerism, ecologist and peace associations. And in the family of course. Where everything begins. Because the emancipation of women is not only a product of the law (which provides for formal equality) but also a matter of behaviour, of attitude, of conviction too.

Bibliography

Georges Duby and Michelle Perrot, *Histoire des femmes. Tome V: Le XXème siècle* (Paris: Plon, 1992).

Susan Faludi, *Backlash, The undeclared war against women – La guerre froide contre les femmes* (Paris: Des Femmes, 1993).

Gisèle Halimi, *Femmes, moitié de la terre, moitié du pouvoir* (Paris: NRF, 1994).

Kathrin Klett and Danielle Yersin (eds), *Die Gleichstellung von Frau und Mann als rechtspolitischer Auftrag / L'égalité entre hommes et femmes – un mandat politique pour le législateur.* (Basel and Frankfurt am Main: Helbing & Lichtenhahn 1993).

Charles-Albert Morand (ed.), *L'égalité entre hommes et femmes – Bilan et perspectives* (Lausanne: Payot, 1988).

Gabrielle Nanchen, *Amour et pouvoir – Des hommes, des femmes et des valeurs* (Lausanne: Favre, 1990).

Lotti Ruckstuhl, *Vers la majorité politique – Histoire du suffrage féminin en Suisse* (Zürich/Lausanne: Interfeminas/ADF, 1990).

Claire Torracinta-Pache, *Le pouvoir est pour demain – Les femmes dans la politique suisse* (Lausanne: L'Aire, 1984).

Inge Volk, *Gibt es eine weibliche Politik? – Gespräche mit Politikerinnen* (Berlin: Quadriga, 1992).

OECD, *Les femmes et la ville. Logements, services et environnement urbain* (Paris: 1995).

Contributors

AGNÈS CARDINAL (1942) was born in Zurich and studied first in Switzerland and then in Britain. Since 1978 she has taught German at the University of Kent and has published extensively on Robert Walser and women writers in Germany and Switzerland.

JOY CHARNLEY (1960) first became interested in the literature of *Suisse romande* when she was living in La Chaux-de-Fonds. Since taking up a post in French at the University of Strathclyde she has pursued this interest in both her teaching and research and has published articles on Yvette Z'Graggen and women in Switzerland.

ANNE CUNEO (1936) is Italian by birth but has lived in Switzerland since the 1940s, first in Lausanne and now in Zurich. She has worked in journalism and the theatre and published her first book in 1967. She was awarded the Prix Schiller in 1980 and her new novel, *Objets de splendeur. Mr Shakespeare amoureux* appeared in autumn 1996.

ANNELIES DEBRUNNER (1949) worked as a primary-school teacher until 1982 when she began her studies at the University of Zurich, where she obtained her doctorate in 1993. She is now a sociologist, has worked on a series of research projects and published in the field of women and work and women's lives.

YVETTE JAGGI (1941) has been politically active since 1979, both locally and nationally, becoming Mayor of Lausanne in 1990. She has also been very involved in the area of consumer rights, as President of the *Fédération romande des consommatrices* from 1973 to 1979 and has expressed her views in works such as *Ce n'est pas le moment de mollir* (1991).

LIZ LOCHHEAD (1947) studied art and qualified as a teacher before becoming a full-time writer in 1978. She has written plays, poetry and film scripts, and her many publications include *Blood and Ice, Mary Queen of Scots Got her Head Chopped off* and *Quelques Fleurs*.

BEATRICE VON MATT studied in Zurich, Paris and Cambridge and wrote for many years on literature for the *Neue Zürcher Zeitung*. Recognised as a leading specialist on German-Swiss literature, she has published extensively, including *Antworten: Die Literatur der deutschsprachigen Schweiz in den achtziger Jahren* which appeared in 1991.

ELISABETTA PAGNOSSIN ALIGISAKIS (1954) is a political scientist who works in the field of women's participation in politics. In addition to her work on a research project in Geneva looking at the status of housework, she is preparing a book which will study the role of women in the European parliament.

MALCOLM PENDER (1935) has taught German at the University of Strathclyde since 1964. He has published several important monographs on German-Swiss literature and a further work on *Sickness and Death in Contemporary German-Swiss Writing* is due to appear in 1997.

PATRICIA PLATTNER (1953) studied visual arts in Geneva and worked in graphics for some years before making her first short feature in 1986. She formed her own production company, Light Night Productions, in 1988 and has gone on to make several more films, including *Piano Panier* (1989) and *Hôtel Abyssinie* (1996).

AMÉLIE PLUME (1943) lives in Geneva and has published seven books since 1981, the most recent being *Hélas, nos chéris sont nos ennemis* (1995). In 1988 she was awarded the Prix Schiller.

ISOLDE SCHAAD (1944) who lives in Zurich, is a freelance journalist and author who has also worked in theatre and radio. Her work includes *Die Zürcher Constipation* (1986) and *Body und Sofa* (1994).

ROSEMARIE SIMMEN (1938) qualified as a pharmacist and worked in this capacity for several years before taking time off to bring up her children. In 1983 she was elected to the parliament of the Canton of Solothurn and in 1987 she became a member of the Swiss Upper House. Since 1990 she has also been President of Pro Helvetia.

BRIGITTE STUDER (1955) divides her time between Zurich, where she teaches, and Lausanne, where she is involved in a research project. She has published in the field of women's studies and is also a specialist on the Swiss Communist party. In 1994 she published *Un parti sous influence. Le parti communiste suisse 1931–1939.*

ERIKA SWALES (1937) studied in Switzerland, the USA and Britain before settling in Cambridge where she is now a Fellow of King's College. She has published extensively, in particular on Kleist and Keller.

REGINA WECKER (1944) was born in Berlin, where she studied for some years before moving to Basle. She has taught history at the university there since the 1970s and is now a leading specialist on women's and gender history, with publications on women's rights in the workplace, and the writing of women's history.

ANDREW WILKIN (1944) has taught Italian at the University of Strathclyde since 1967. He is editor of the journal *Tuttitalia* and has published articles on Italian-Swiss literature.